ABROAD AND BEYOND

Abroad and beyond

Patterns in American overseas education

A study sponsored by The Institute of International Education

CRAUFURD D. GOODWIN

Duke University

and

MICHAEL NACHT

University of Maryland

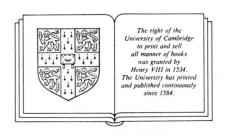

The right of the
University of Cambridge
to print and sell
all manner of books
was granted by
Henry VIII in 1534.
The University has printed
and published continuously
since 1584.

CAMBRIDGE UNIVERSITY PRESS

Cambridge

New York   New Rochelle   Melbourne   Sydney

Published by the Press Syndicate of the University of Cambridge
The Pitt Building, Trumpington Street, Cambridge CB2 1RP
32 East 57th Street, New York, NY 10022, USA
10 Stamford Road, Oakleigh, Melbourne 3166, Australia

First published 1988

Printed in Canada

Library of Congress Cataloging-in-Publication Data
Goodwin, Craufurd, D. W.
Abroad and beyond : patterns in American overseas education /
Craufurd D. Goodwin and Michael Nacht.
p. cm.
Includes index.
ISBN 0 521 35463 3. ISBN 0 521 35742 X (pbk.)
1. Foreign study. 2. American students – Foreign countries.
I. Nacht, Michael. II. Title.
LB2376.G66 1988
370.19′6 – dc19 87–27751

British Library Cataloguing in Publication Data
Goodwin, Craufurd D.
Abroad and beyond : patterns in American overseas education.
1. Foreign Study 2. American students in foreign countries
I. Title II. Nacht, Michael
378′.35 LB2376
ISBN 0 521 35463 3

Contents

Preface

In 1982 we completed a study of policy toward foreign students in American colleges and universities entitled *Absence of Decision* (IIE, 1982). This was followed by two further studies: One addressed the impact of an American higher education on foreign students (*Fondness and Frustration*, IIE, 1983), and the other examined the long-term intellectual and professional difficulties faced by these students when they returned home (*Decline and Renewal*, IIE, 1986). In these works our approach has been to identify and lay out for consideration problems and issues discovered in conversations with practitioners and policymakers. We have not ourselves had deep involvement with any of the programs under review and therefore we bring to our tasks a mixture of innocence and detachment.

In this study we examine the other side of the foreign student question – policies and programs for American students venturing overseas. Once more our objective is not to fix praise or blame on programs and policies to date or indeed to prescribe particular change. Instead we wish to lead our readers into and through this large subject of study abroad dwelling upon questions and issues that we find to be of special relevance. Whereas in 1982 we found foreign student policy relatively little attended on campuses, yet crying out for action, in 1986 we discovered that study abroad is a hot topic – perhaps too hot for its own good. We heard positions expressed with remarkable vehemence and intolerance and we encountered relatively little balanced analysis. Contenders argued from different positions on many topics that truth lay only "here" but not "there"; valid points, they argued, could be made on this side of an argument or that, but not on both. As newcomers to the field, and agnostics, we found this condition to be sometimes confusing and, overall, unsatisfactory. We think it should be equally so for others – deans, provosts, presidents, legislators, foundation officers, faculty members – called upon to make policy in the field. Our main goal, therefore, is to sort out the broad subject as it came clear to us over several months of talk and reflection. We hope that, by and large, we have "got it right." We try not to come out decisively on the side of any of the various contending parties in the numerous disputes that rock the field, not because we eschew the role of Solomon but because we usually do see two sides. We try above all to explain what the arguments are, for and against the several positions, so that the reader is then well positioned to draw his/her own conclusions.

Study abroad has come a very long way since the early days of Smith in Geneva, Sweetbriar in Paris, and Yale in China. Now the practice has many more purposes and many more forms. To get one's mind around the subject completely is no easy task. Our approach is, first, to provide a catalog of all the different purposes for study abroad, and of the ways to carry it out. Then we describe a range of specific questions and issues that may arise on the subject on any campus. Finally we describe a few innovative programs at a range of institutions that may, we think, be stimulating to any college or university considering its own activities in the field.

In order to encounter as wide a spectrum of views as possible on study abroad, we visited approximately forty colleges and universities in four states plus a variety of relevant organizations and other interested institutions. We picked California, Illinois, Massachusetts, and Texas because of the great diversity they offered in geography, style, type of institution, and attitude toward our subject. We selected a wide range of institutions, from small liberal arts and two-year colleges to major research universities, public and private, rural and urban, rich and poor, committed to study abroad and largely oblivious to it. We made initial contact with the president of each institution and then spent approximately one half of a day on each campus talking with administrators and faculty with views on the subject. We had a set list of questions to guide the conversation, but typically after outlining the subject we encouraged our hosts to direct the conversation where they would. On several campuses we met celebrated old hands in the study abroad business. In this report we cannot tell them anything they do not know already. We are most grateful to them, and to our other conversation partners during our travels, for providing the grist for our mill.

We came away from our reflections on this subject with the firm conviction that this is, indeed, a subject of great importance to American higher education today, not only because it affords valuable opportunities for students and faculty and because it will bubble and boil whether or not it is attended thoughtfully, but because it involves many fundamental issues in higher education that are reflected here in magnified form. We hope that this analysis will open up the subject effectively for those who are only peripherally acquainted with it. For those who are more deeply involved we trust this review will yield some unexpected questions and some insights that are new.

This project was made possible by grants from the Andrew W. Mellon and Alfred P. Sloan foundations. We are grateful to both for their support and encouragement. Elinor Barber, our colleague at the Institute of International Education (IIE), has been a steady source of support and constructive encouragement. Several experienced leaders of study abroad kindly read and suggested changes in this work: Faire Goldstein of Brandeis University, A. Kenneth Pye of Southern Methodist University, Cassandra Pyle of the Council for International Exchange of Scholars, and Joan Salaun of the University of Illinois. Archer Brown of the National Association for Foreign Student Affairs generously helped us collect material for Chapter 7. We thank each of them for this wise counsel.

1

Introduction

During the 1980s study abroad has attracted an unexpected level of interest and attention in American higher education. There is widespread agreement that the rate of growth has accelerated sharply. Reliable statistics do not exist, however, because neither the federal government nor any private institution collects data systematically about this important subject. Even colleges and universities typically know little about their own campuses. They probably can estimate roughly the numbers enrolled in their own study abroad programs, but when their students study abroad with other institutions they are likely to be shown on educational records only as "on leave"! The growth during the early 1980s in most of the places we visited had been quite startling. We encountered no institution at all where the numbers had declined, and there were many with a compound growth rate of 5–10 percent in a constant student population. Some institutions set goals for participation that varied from 5 to 90 percent of the student body. To give only one rather typical example, in one highly selective private liberal arts college the numbers in study abroad had risen from a negligible six in 1976–7 to seventy-eight in 1985–6, or 16 percent of the junior class in the latter year. At that point it was decided that for financial reasons this proportion should not rise above 20 percent, and the challenge this college now faces is to see how the ever-rising numbers can be constrained.

We typically ended our discussion at an institution by asking what study abroad would be like on the campus we were visiting a decade hence. Most projected confidently substantial growth. In some institutions where study abroad has not been well developed to date we detected an almost alarmist sense of having been left behind and needing to get on the train even though it has already left the station. Projections into the future in these places were based on a belief that it was necessary to catch up from the past. In institutions where growth has been headlong there was also deep concern, but in these cases it centered on keeping track of the activities that had grown up.

The proportion of students on the campuses we visited who had taken part in some kind of study program abroad varied from negligible to more than half, so there is still substantial room for growth at many institutions. Several colleges outside of those states we visited, as well as one we did visit, have a commitment to virtually full participation of undergraduates in study abroad. The innumerable reforms of undergraduate curriculum now being effected on many campuses typically prescribe a significant role for study abroad.

Chief executives of colleges and universities, because of the breadth of their perspectives, are often the best barometer of fashion. Consequently the large number of times internationalization of the institution is expressed currently as a goal in presidential and deanly rhetoric reflects to a considerable degree the extent to which study abroad has become embraced at the highest levels.

A growth stock in a stagnant industry

Why then this remarkable growth and projections of an even more rosy future? A number of reasons emerged in our conversations.

It seems reasonable to place first a new yearning by the young of America to understand the world in which they live. They cannot help but be conscious today that their prosperity and indeed their very survival depend on knowing and developing sound relations with their neighbors. However, while the media bombard the youth with accounts of international terrorism, hostage-taking, guerrilla wars, grain embargos, trade competition, and anti-Americanism, their educational system equips them very little to explain these events. The high schools do practically nothing at all. At the college level the social sciences and humanities seem arid and irrelevant;

area studies reach undergraduates in limited ways and seem burdened with esoterica. Study abroad has become the place where students can get hands-on contact with the world and where they may turn for understanding.

The second reason for the growth is the decreasing cost of foreign study as the dollar grew stronger during the early 1980s. This, combined with steadily rising costs of higher education in the United States, has sent students looking for bargains. American students and their families have simply done in their purchases of higher education what they have done in other consumption patterns: substituted cheaper (and perhaps higher quality) imports for more expensive (and less attractive) American products.

Third, American society's views of other nations seem to have softened in recent years. After the trauma of Vietnam, Americans of all ages today seem to want to reach out and live peacefully with others. They realize now that there are no easy answers in a complex world. Their sense of an urgent need to know has been accentuated by the feeling that traditional foreign policy in this century has kept us on the road to disaster and may have us there still. It is necessary to understand our neighbors in personal, human terms, to search for alternatives to military conflict, and to seek to resolve differences. The area studies style of the 1960s, in which a few faculty experts and their graduate students came to know foreign lands intimately and passed this knowledge on to undergraduates and others, has lost much of its appeal in the 1980s. Students mistrust the humanities and social sciences as filters to understanding the world: They want to be there and experience it themselves. In a way the rising popularity of study abroad reflects a growing faith in the power of the senses to facilitate understanding.

Fourth, by the 1980s foreign travel had become so familiar to so many Americans, either as tourists or through service in the armed forces, the Peace Corps, or a multinational corporation, that it seemed only natural to carry this mobile life-style over to higher education – and unnatural not to do so. Related to this changed gestalt surrounding mobility, not only in the United States but other western nations as well, is the pervasiveness of a new international youth culture in which the peripatetic student feels almost as comfortable in one country as in another. Thirty years ago there were few cities in which a foreign student could blend easily and be accepted – Paris and a few university towns, perhaps. Today students find it almost as easy to "hang out" in Madrid, or even Kathmandu, as in London or Rome. The itinerant youth of the late twentieth century forming bonds across national boundaries constitute a universalist subculture the significance of which is only just being explored. Clearly, study abroad is for some American students more than a strictly educational experience: It is a ticket to short-term membership in this subculture.

The cultural metamorphosis of students, which is easier to sense than to measure, may have been in effect long enough to be reflected by young faculty as well. It seemed to us that, even discounting for age, sympathy toward study abroad was markedly greater among faculty trained during the 1960s and 1970s than in earlier decades.

The full generational aspect of study abroad is just beginning to make itself felt. The children and even the grandchildren of study abroad alumni are highly enthusiastic applicants, according to schools, like Smith College, that have been in the business a very long time. The children of Peace Corps volunteers are also already a visible presence. It may be that when the children of the burgeoning study-abroaders of the 1980s appear on the scene a truly explosive growth may occur.

It is important not to leave the impression that in the mid-1980s study abroad is carrying all before it on the campuses. There remains a good deal of indifference in some quarters and a high level of skepticism, even hostility, among many faculty, administrators, and friends of higher education. Their concerns take three forms:

1. They doubt the rigor and seriousness of the academic programs. Moreover, they fear that provisions for quality control are inadequate in most respects.
2. They mistrust the motives that lead their colleagues to pursue program development. We heard often terms like "fac-

ulty frolic," and "lucrative playpens." On campuses where study abroad was currently in bad odor, faculty attitudes were said to be a mixture of "ignorance, disinterest, suspicion, hostility, and the conviction that it was all just an irrelevant distraction on the road to professional careers."

3. They believe the students' time could be used better at home; they regret the loss of their own courses, the "breaking of the major" for the junior year, and the implication that the best of all worlds cannot be found on the home campus.

A good deal of the skepticism of study abroad is based, we conclude, on a rather careless assumption that it is still simply the grand tour for the well-to-do ("fine for a rich private college, but not for us") rather than a valuable, or even vital, feature of higher education. This belief explains symbolic rules in one state university prohibiting use of public funds for foreign travel, or even for transoceanic phone calls! A vital need, we suggest, is to persuade these critics to reflect at least upon the variety of important potential accomplishments of study abroad discussed in Chapter 3. Institutions of higher education tend to be concerned as much with respectability as with other virtues. If they find that study abroad verges on the disreputable, we suggest that further careful reflection may change this perception. Nevertheless, it is important to understand this skepticism both as an element of the environment in which study abroad must evolve and for the truth it may contain.

From the reports we received the governing boards of colleges and universities have been generally supportive of, but usually not deeply interested in, study abroad. To the extent they offer comment it is to endorse an activity that recognizes and facilitates the internationalization of the institution, and of the society of which it is a part.

Reflections of large issues in higher education

A variety of other circumstances, including the effects of electronic media in creating a "global village," combined to make study abroad both a field for action and a topic for vigorous discussion on most campuses during our visits in 1986. Strikingly it turns out that a probing exploration of the subject leads quickly to a range of questions that are central to much of higher education today. At the very front is the question of what a liberal education is all about. Can it be defined as the mastery of a set of subjects and courses, or does it involve above all personal growth of the students? If the latter, can such qualities as personal maturity and sensitivity, extension of perspective, and appreciation and tolerance of difference, be identified and measured? And if they can indeed be measured, perhaps through a proxy, should college "credit" be awarded for their acquisition? As a related question, should professional training (of lawyers, doctors, engineers, etc.) be distinguished starkly from that of the student of the liberal arts? Is it only the social scientist or humanist who "needs" a sophisticated appreciation of the world? If not, how can "liberalization" on a global scale be carried over to the natural and physical sciences and the professional schools so that their products may be not only more skilled but better educated in the largest sense? Is a scientist and professional "trained," or is he/she too "educated," that is, taught not merely how to perform a task but how to visualize and comprehend the task in the widest possible sense? Regardless of the actual content of the curriculum, the self-perception of either education or training is a crucial distinction. Given that study abroad may not contribute directly to much scientific or professional training, does it not perhaps have a vital role in "educating" the young scientist and professional? It was suggested to us by one engineer that while pressure for more study abroad at the moment was coming from undergraduates in the humanities and the social sciences, the future lay in professional areas. He discerned that narrow professionalization was beginning to lose its luster with the faculty, and disillusionment would move gradually back to the students, who thus far were very tightly disciplined and inclined to accept what was prescribed for them. If nothing else the very high quality of professional students today should reduce their docility on the question of overseas study.

Issues of governance in higher education arise immediately in discussion of study abroad. Who should inspire and guide this activity on campus? Do authority and responsibility lie most appropriately with the faculty member, or the administering departments, or the school? Or can study abroad be seen most sensibly as of institutional concern, like the football team or library, and therefore become the charge of the central administration? Is study abroad part of the basic mission of an institution or is it an appendage that can be indulged during prosperity and then sacrificed in hard times? Should it perhaps be left to a student affairs division to be handled like the student union? Whence should the precise leadership and impetus for change come: from department chairpersons, deans, and/or presidents? Or from individual faculty members? Should the demands of students for change be attended in this case, or can it be assumed that students do not know their best interests? Is this perhaps an educational activity that may satisfactorily be contracted to an outside agency, like food services, rather than be seen as the teaching of history or mathematics, which must be conducted internally? What should be the proper relationship between administrators charged to oversee study abroad and faculty charged to operate the programs? Is one properly the master and the other the servant? What are effective devices in this case to maintain quality control? Should study abroad be required to break even financially, make money, or lose no more than a specified charge on endowment and public funds?

Consideration of study abroad also leads quickly into questions of the appropriate constituency for higher education. Is study abroad most properly reserved for a select few? If so, which few, and why place greater limitations in this area than in others? To a large extent the question of constituency has not been answered; to the extent that it has, this has been by the students themselves. Whereas only a few years ago study abroad was confined almost exclusively to liberal arts colleges and to a few graduate departments, now it is fair game for just about anyone, from the part-time elderly retiree at an urban community college to the promising young computer scientist at the selective technical institute. The challenge to develop appropriately heterogeneous programs for such a varied constituency is enormous. Where this expansion will lead is unclear but its own momentum is presently carrying it forward at a considerable pace.

The place of structure in the university curriculum, especially at the undergraduate level, has been vigorously debated on campuses throughout the 1980s. Should the wide freedom of choice introduced mainly in the 1960s be constrained in the interest of the student consumers? Should old requirements be restored or new ones introduced? A language requirement and responsibility for familiarity with a foreign culture are often topics of debate, and in both cases study abroad is clearly relevant. Overseas experience has played a part in both language and area studies over the years; the point now is whether today it might do more.

The question is often asked whether higher education varies widely in different parts of the United States, corrected for such other variables as degree of urbanization. Our impressions are that, with respect to study abroad, differences are real and important, reflecting presumably the attitudes of residents of the campuses more than physical realities. It appears from our sample of four states that, for the most part, on the two coasts study abroad has a longer history and deeper traditions than in the interior of the nation. In the West there seems an especially strong sense of urgency to make it happen, while in the East the attitude is more relaxed, as if it can be assumed students will go abroad sometime and somehow and the matter need not receive much attention. (Harvard University, for example, reports that 60 percent of its students will have worked or studied abroad, one way or another, within five years of matriculation.) In the Midwest and Southwest we found most often a sentiment that study abroad was a comparatively new phenomenon with special relevance to their region's increasing involvement in world affairs.

In the chapters that follow we examine many of these large questions related to study abroad, just as we attempt to understand the growth and progress of the overseas study movement.

2

The point of it all

An argument made, often forcefully and convincingly, by those experienced in international educational exchange, is that programs of study abroad will almost certainly fail if their particular goals are not specified carefully and kept clearly in mind by their operators. For this reason we began to compile a list of the various purposes for which programs we discussed had evidently been created. It is possible, of course, and by no means inappropriate for a single program to have several purposes at the same time; this simply complicates the operation. It is more common for multiple purposes to be addressed by multiple programs, across the nation but also within individual institutions. Some of the purposes we discerned seemed overlapping, some complementary, and some potentially contradictory. The planners and operators of programs did not, of course, construct all of them with well-formulated goals explicitly stated; but in virtually all cases one or more of the purposes we list below can, at a minimum, be seen peeping out of obscurity. Some few programs, we saw, may truly never have had a purpose: They just grew. Their survival, it is clear, will always be in great peril.

The list that follows is not necessarily complete. However, it does seem to cover the objectives of the several hundred programs we explored and discussed. The list is divided into two parts for convenience: first, educational and social goals, then institutional and administrative goals. This is not to suggest a predetermined hierarchy among the goals, nor is it intended that any of them should be seen as inherently illegitimate, even if some do seem to lack the lofty objectives customarily associated with higher education. Nor is it suggested that a particular set of goals can easily be prescribed for any institution: Each institution has its own values and needs and its own constraints; a legitimate purpose for one may not fit another. What follows, then, is a checklist of possible goals for study abroad that any institution would be well advised to review – if for no other reason than to clarify its own purposes and recall other opportunities.

Educational and social goals and potential accomplishments

1. The "finishing school" and the "grand tour"

An honored tradition of western culture, going back even to the ancient Greeks, is to acquaint the children of privileged families with an extended range of cultural experience. To become "cultured" citizens, it has long been believed, young people must have some acquaintance with and understanding of the arts, sights, and sounds of other peoples. It is difficult for this to be done entirely at home. Moreover, through personal contacts made abroad the privileged young may even become part of a cosmopolitan and international social set. Of all purposes for study abroad this has the longest history. The celebrated grand tour of young British aristocrats, sometimes accompanied by distinguished tutors (such as Adam Smith with the children of the Duke of Buccleuch), and the twentieth-century Swiss finishing schools for wealthy young women of all nations were in this tradition. The evident purpose implicit in this goal is inculcation of cultural attributes appropriate for a particular social class and station. A collateral purpose may be to provide the tools for a genteel occupation such as language teaching. This particular goal, stated boldly as it is here, is currently out of fashion with American students and their families. It cannot be proclaimed explicitly. However, informally it remains intact, lurking in the shadows, especially at some more expensive liberal arts colleges and private universities. It might be argued that study abroad as acculturation for privileged youth has been retained by American higher education to some extent but has been democratized and made available to the middle class.

2. *Broadening the intellectual élite*

This goal is to create, as nearly as possible, truly multicultural individuals, who will lead society in all its parts: business, government, the professions, education, and so on. Whereas the previous goal is intended to provide a veneer, this goal is to change the entire human being. Early pursuers of this goal were the young American pioneers of higher education who, during the second half of the nineteenth century, enrolled in the great German universities. Even earlier progenitors were the peripatetic scholars of medieval and Renaissance Europe, epitomized by the wanderer Erasmus. The principles behind the Rhodes Scholars Program fall in this category. Such complete commitment by highly qualified students is the goal of study abroad that many American academics find most agreeable. It requires hard work and sacrifice, and virtually by definition it excludes the faint of heart and weak of mind. Pursuit of this goal is often referred to as a privilege, an honors program, and a badge of accomplishment for those who achieve it successfully.

A changing feature of this goal relates to an evolving conception of the nature of the élite in the United States and of the relationship of world affairs to it. During the interwar years and before, that part of the leadership cadre for which knowledge of the world was thought to be relevant was roughly those destined for a career in the higher reaches of government and the foreign service, together with those few who would assume positions of authority throughout society based on a broad liberal education. Those who performed "service" roles as engineers, lawyers, doctors, hard scientists, accountants, and even senior business managers need not concern themselves with happenings offshore. The postwar decades have deeply shaken this assumption, and persons in or destined for senior positions throughout American life have concluded that they too must reach out to study and understand the larger world. Their personal security, economic interests, leadership responsibilities, and even their professional careers have less and less meaning when viewed from a narrow national perspective. Yet the structures for training in these applied fields have little place for this

wider perspective. Some of the most interesting and exciting developments in study abroad today relate to efforts by the more
visionary educational leaders in these professional areas to develop
viable and effective means to give their charges a sophisticated
understanding of the world in which they live. We were struck by
the range of complex unexpected results that these leaders perceived could be gained by their students from a foreign educational
experience. In some cases it was a new perspective on their professional material; in others it was a source of creative inspiration.
We expect that many more such effects will be discovered in the
years just ahead.

3. *Internationalizing the educated citizenry*

The justification used for the largest number of study abroad programs today is that any exposure to a foreign environment during
one's formal education is better than none. Students will be faced
overseas with "difference." The defenders of this goal speak especially of a personal metamorphosis in those who partake – a
gestalt change that varies with the individual, cannot be predicted
in detail, but is enormously important as an outcome. Students in
this way become, it is said, more mature, sophisticated, hungry
for knowledge, culturally aware, and sensitive. They learn by ques-
tioning their own prejudices and all national stereotypes. They ask
the meaning of national culture. Their horizons are extended and
they gain new perspectives. Critics of this goal say it simply cannot
be achieved, while futile attempts to do so may jeopardize truly
important goals like goal 2.

Many advocates of study abroad see a major element of educational remediation in this goal. The American educational systems of secondary and higher education, they say, have been simply
derelict in imbuing most of their charges with even the most rudimentary understanding of the rest of the planet on which they
reside. After years of nominal language study they are seldom able
even to order a meal overseas, and they are barely able to find
the United States on the globe, let alone distinguish Austria from
Australia. The ignorance of "place geography" is legendary. At

one highly selective liberal arts college we were told of a student inquiring what language was spoken in Italy, and of another declining to study in Denmark "because her parents would not let her live in South America." It is argued that with the powerful continental culture of the United States, and with its strong monolingual tradition, direct insertion in a foreign culture is the only way to provide the cosmopolitan qualities expected in an educated person.

Understandably we heard the most moving accounts of the sea change wrought in individual students when we traveled farthest from each coast. In the Southwest we were told of students arriving at two large public universities who had never seen an escalator: A tour of Austin or College Station alone was a real adventure. Four months spent in Paris two years later were simply mind-boggling. In large measure what we were repeatedly told was this: For many students from the American hinterland an overseas educational experience broadened their perspectives in unimaginable ways, for they were now able to appreciate the extraordinary heterogeneity of human society and the powerful influence exerted by culture on institutions. It was only through study abroad that they began to question the notion that "they're just like us."

4. Fulfillment of a distinctive institutional mission

Some colleges and universities find that study abroad is a means to respond to some specific local institutional imperative. This is especially true of church-related colleges, which combine a concern for service and adherence to doctrine with an essential international dimension. For example, the University of Dallas, a Catholic university, offers a one-semester program in Rome for sophomores as a valuable foundation for later learning. (See Chapter 6.) Baylor, a Baptist-related university, on the other hand, has adapted its long missionary experience in Asia and Africa to emphasize service-related study abroad, especially through internships of various kinds. A current example is a nursing-service program in China.

5. *To explore our roots*

As an immigrant society America finds most of its population looking overseas somewhere to find forebears, family, and a cultural heritage. Many study abroad programs were established and have prospered in pursuit of this goal. Students who, like Henry Adams, beat a path back to Europe only a few years after the American Revolution were driven by a mixture of nostalgia, loneliness, and a desire to understand oneself through contact with the extended family. More recent programs in Poland, Japan, Ireland, Canada, Taiwan, Israel, and many other places can be traced directly to this impetus. But the circumstances faced by "roots" programs can be more complex than first they seem. For example, America also shares the myth of the melting pot, and not all children of immigrants wish to be reminded too vividly of their parents' origins. It was suggested to us that third and later generations of children are usually more interested in returning to the homeland than children of actual immigrants. Another complication with these programs is that the seemingly most promising candidates for them are also those most likely to have visited as tourists and not to want to go again. We encountered programs in Israel and Ireland that had not prospered for exactly this reason ("I spent a summer on a kibbutz, why spend a college year as well?"). Furthermore, children of immigrants are likely to have uncles and aunts and cousins in the old country who may constrain the sense of independence and adventure that is among the most attractive features of the study abroad experience. There is also the well-known embarrassment felt by students with names and physical appearance the same as those of the natives of the country in which they are studying, but who are unable to speak the language fluently or recall all the cultural rules. It is worth remembering that ambitious programs with an overwhelming roots objective have failed under the most promising conditions at institutions we visited. It is important to note also that, of course, by no means all the study abroad conducted in countries where Americans have roots has this objective in view.

6. *Master a foreign language*

Mastery of a modern language has traditionally been perceived as the most direct educational benefit of study abroad. A foreign language, say its advocates, is not merely a tool and a key to both scholarly inquiry and to commercial success; it is also the main route to cultural understanding. So long as visitors are cut off from the language of a people they will see them, indeed, through a glass darkly. With a period of residency overseas students are not only provided with a relatively painless total involvement in the language, but they are able also to see romance and excitement in it that could not be imparted by even the best classroom study. We did encounter a few language teachers who claimed that foreign languages could better be taught at home without all the "impure" distractions of an overseas setting; but the overwhelming conclusion was to the contrary. Overseas the variety of linguistic opportunities is unlimited while the "need to know" is everywhere around. Some language departments claim success in reaching practical fluency in as little as six weeks of total commitment overseas. They report also a substantial increase of new majors (often second majors) from among those who study abroad. At least one language department made study abroad an absolute requirement of their majors.

We encountered some interesting controversy, however, over the purpose of language study abroad. In contrast to those in language departments who typically seek sophisticated command of syntax and literature, faculty in professional schools of business and engineering look to facility in conversation or "street language." One said "You can buy in English but you can't sell in English. That's what we care about, not reading great works of literature." Another, talking about learning Chinese, suggested that from his perspective a fair test of success in language skills was whether the student could carry on a rich discussion with a noodle vendor.

The critics of study abroad for language training come from two directions. One group argues that time spent abroad is too precious to be dominated by a focus on language: Fluency can be gained at home whereas other overseas experience cannot. This group gives priority to one or more of the other goals discussed in this chapter and holds that a language orientation, and especially domination of study abroad programs by language departments, places them in serious jeopardy.

The other critics say that huge opportunities are being lost today to fulfil the new language requirements being introduced on many campuses through low-cost, high-speed language instruction for masses of students. Language departments, these critics charge, are concerned excessively with their majors and not enough with the mass of others who must fulfil a requirement. One visionary claimed that a truly imaginative program during ten weeks on a Mexican campus could provide the equivalent of three years of language instruction in the United States. A shuttle of 747s into Guadalajara with monolinguals and out with bilinguals would, in his view, bring benefits to all.

It was interesting to hear from the chairman of one language department that study abroad presented special problems by generating students too advanced for his upper-division courses.

7. The world as a laboratory

Some fields like art history and architecture can barely envisage serious commitments to their subjects without sustained overseas experience. For the former, direct exposure to the great works of art finds no substitute in the slide projector. The giants of design – Frank Lloyd Wright, Mies van der Rohe, Le Corbusier – all traveled widely, experiencing "spaces and places," and these inspirational examples are not lost on their followers. Both artists and architects with whom we talked thought a major shift in the wanderings in their professions would occur soon away from the traditional haunts of Western Europe to Asia, Africa, and Latin America. To those who argue that there is little of relevance outside the First World one architect replied, "An imaginative person can find much of relevance, a dull person never can." He gave as one "relevant" instance the insights that should come from a careful study of energy-efficient Asian cities to any Western architect who will practice in the twenty-first century.

It is hard to conceive how today, with the ready availability of study abroad opportunities, such specialized subfields as international relations and international business, or such interdisciplinary majors as international and comparative studies, can fail to prescribe "laboratory" trips overseas – and indeed more and more institutions are doing so. If necessary the cost of study abroad in this mode can be kept to a minimum by providing instruction at home and only the fieldwork or inspection of evidence and illustration overseas.

Many new fields are coming to conclude, to one degree or another, that unique benefits may accrue from teaching in a foreign "laboratory." The social sciences, their commitment to sophisticated method and technique beginning to cool, find new excitement in a return to the comparative study of social institutions. Some colleges distinguish between study abroad for "liberal education," meaning goals 1–3 in this list, and for "enriching the major." It is under this latter heading that the world as a locus for fieldwork becomes important. Study abroad in this sense changes not the student but rather the materials under study.

8. To know ourselves

A theme we heard often during our campus visits was that to understand ourselves and our nation in the late twentieth century it is necessary to move beyond our borders. We must listen to the insights of foreign observers and must benefit from the fresh perspectives that come to us from detachment. This objective for study abroad seems to be rooted in three different positions. First, some believe that America has fundamentally lost its way and must reconceive its place in the world. Hubris, it is argued, has led the American people astray and only close contact with the rest of the world will set them on the right path again. A second argument is that certain relationships, and the U.S. role in them – for example, Third World dependency – can be appreciated only by experience on the spot. Moreover, for the negotiations with other parts of the world that must surely increase in the years ahead we must understand not only our negotiating partners but their perceptions of us as well. The third argument is less suffused with political doctrine: It claims that virtually all the social sciences and humanities must have resort to multinational data. A professor of political science went so far as to suggest that a deep appreciation of American government itself cannot be gained entirely within; it requires some time spent outside looking in. The "Robert Burns effect" – the gift to see ourselves as others see us – comes to social scientists and humanists overseas.

9. Learn from others

A widespread belief among American academics for some years after World War II was that this country stood far ahead in virtually all disciplines and would remain so into the foreseeable future. American scholars went abroad to give rather than to receive, to teach but not to learn. Increasingly this belief is being displaced today by widespread wonder at scholarly achievements overseas: Japan in engineering (e.g., robotics and appropriate technology), Western Europe in particle physics, the Soviet Union in mathematics. The challenge remains to discover how American students may best connect with those fields abroad in which this country now lags. The two systems of instruction are not easily integrated, especially in technical fields, and the most promising linkages may remain at the more senior levels. But the goal of tapping the increasingly rich foreign veins of intellectual talent remains a compelling one, and is perhaps the goal growing most rapidly in interest at this time.

We encountered some of the most stark contrasts of view in discussions of this goal, and we suspect that in many institutions the need for full discussion and arrival at a consensus is greatest here. For example, some engineers at leading schools argued that great strides were now made abroad in fields of great importance to the United States but of which Americans were largely ignorant. They claimed that in areas like robotics and manufacturing Japanese engineers were well ahead, but much of the literature in

Japanese is unavailable to monolingual Americans. They urged the education of a new generation of American engineers with facility in non-Western languages and the cultural sophistication to permit the growth of international personal ties. We heard the same arguments made for business administration, design, and a range of other areas. But on the other side of this argument we heard it said confidently that English had now finally become the lingua franca of science and technology, and any discoveries worthy of attention would turn up in due time in English at international conferences and in the international literature. From this perspective ignorance of a foreign language becomes effectively an economizing device that permits a scientist or engineer to ignore inferior contributions and limit his attention to those that survive the critical screen and emerge triumphantly into English. It was impossible for us to adjudicate between these two positions but we are certain that their resolution is most important for the national interest. We must confess to feeling rather more sympathy in general for the advocates of internationalizing the sciences and professional areas, if for no other reason than because of the evident naïveté of the critics in some of their comments. When we asked a senior administrator of one prominent Midwestern business school, surrounded as he was by crumbling American manufacturing industry, whether his students might learn anything from the Japanese, he said he couldn't think of anything. To prove his point he said "We couldn't have anything to learn from them or they wouldn't send their students to us!" This business school, instead of turning its eyes east, had established exchanges only with the United Kingdom and France, on the ground that this was where the students wish to go. As one ponders trade statistics and comparative rates of GNP growth one wonders whether perhaps this posture is not now appropriate only for *Alice in Wonderland*.

One especially thoughtful engineer suggested to us that study abroad might not be as useful for picking up major discoveries as for finding out in a general way what others are up to and how they are doing it. What is their agenda, their style, their point of view, their atmosphere? He thought scientists should endeavor to attach themselves for a period abroad to a single exciting short-term mentor and worry less about the overall quality of a program or foreign institution. Even for this, of course, they required language facility and cultural sophistication.

As American trade deficits soar in the 1980s a national debate over productivity and competitiveness rages. One suggestion for remedial action is "protection" – isolation of the American economy from the rest of the world. Another approach is to get to know the rest of the world and to beat them at their own games. In this more promising latter strategy overseas study by scientists, engineers, business managers, and other professionals is of singular importance.

10. Improve international relations

To an important degree organized study abroad began in America after World War I in the hope that, thereby, chances for world peace would be increased. Undoubtedly the isolationism and xenophobia that characterized much opinion during the war, and then rejection of the League of Nations afterward, contributed to the sense that knowledge of the world was crucial to formation of sound foreign policy in future. After World War II the impetus for study abroad was accelerated by the sense of a descending mantle of leadership and of unpreparedness for it. If America was indeed to assume the coordinating roles of former imperial powers, its people must understand that which was to be coordinated. This "need to know" in world affairs prompted among other things the establishment of the Fulbright Program and its continued funding over four decades. Hope for achievement of world peace through study abroad rested entirely on intuition and informed common sense – and so it remains today. There is no compelling evidence that well-traveled persons, or those with extended residence overseas, are more likely than those who stay home to adopt or accept more enlightened foreign policies; but it seems likely that they will.

We did not encounter any institution for which this goal was the dominant or overriding one. However it was present in many of our discussions, and it remains important, we suspect, especially for some faculty.

Institutional and administrative goals and potential accomplishments

11. Attract more students

Despite the gloomy demographic forecasts for the population of higher education in the 1980s many of the colleges and universities we visited experience instead an embarrassment of riches in their applicant pools. These "hot" schools find their challenge is how to say "no" rather than in finding enough to whom to say "yes." But this was not true of all! Especially among the smaller, regionally oriented, liberal arts colleges there was a sense of deep foreboding about enrollments and a willingness to try anything that might increase the number of paying customers and thereby improve the bottom line. They conceded to us that study abroad was a doubtful instrument in this struggle for bodies. There were three ways in which study abroad might pay off.

(a) Making the school seem more glamorous, cosmopolitan, and up-to-date might induce more students to enroll as freshmen.
(b) Through such programs overseas, tuition-paying foreign students might be identified and recruited.
(c) Students from other institutions who could be attracted simply to take part in a study abroad program might then be proselytized to transfer to the sponsoring college for the senior year at home.

The faculties and administrations of these colleges seeking enrollments recognized full well the investment and the gamble involved. Not only were commitments of scarce academic dollars and labor required but provision of a viable minimum critical mass in new overseas programs dictated the delivery of scarce upper-division students just at the time when their numbers on the home campus were already becoming distressingly thin. The philosophy had to be "bread upon the waters," but they were unable to repress some dark fears that it would never return manyfold, and that it would simply be eaten by hungry fish.

An important question of principle for any college that uses the availability of study abroad as a recruiting tool is whether it can in good conscience then turn around and impose on those who are permitted to go abroad a selective screen finer than that for the original college admission decision.

12. Attract the best students

We heard repeatedly that, at the undergraduate level at least, an appetizing range of study abroad opportunities, either through local programs or those of other institutions, has become essential for attraction of the most highly recruited students from American high schools. We were told by an admissions director that a survey of national merit scholarship applicants to one university showed financial aid, honors programs, and study abroad as the matters of greatest concern. The hierarchy at another school was number of books in the library, coed dorms, and study abroad. Whether the best students are necessarily those who ultimately take advantage of study abroad opportunities is not clear; but evidently they expect the opportunities to be available. Several institutions have included a study abroad component in their most attractive merit-based scholarship packages. One senior administrator suggested that the accepted profile of a good liberal arts college has now come unequivocally to include study abroad: This, he said, is simply a fact of life that colleges must accept if they wish to compete. We must report, however, that several major research universities, with distinguished undergraduate colleges, contradicted this statement for their own situation and denied that study abroad has any appreciable place in their recruiting. It appears that study abroad is beginning to enter professional schools as a recruiting tool as well as at the undergraduate liberal arts college. Some business, law, journalism, and even engineering schools are starting to advertise opportunities overseas; but this limited flow of material to postgraduate students is still far from the undergraduate flood tide that is so widely visible. We found very little evidence that overseas study is used for recruiting purposes in the Ph.D.-granting graduate schools, traditionally the most conservative units on campus. Overseas research for the dissertation is still expected in some fields but there are few imaginative programs to integrate instruction with overseas research or to develop other devices to make foreign study easier and more valuable. We speculated that innovative study abroad options, especially during the period of course work, might be an effective recruiting device for those graduate schools without other evidences of comparative advantage. But such schemes would remove graduate students from campus just at the time when graduate faculty feel they must receive the whole "truth" as determined locally, and there was not much resonance for this idea.

13. Accede to the entrepreneurial drives of faculty

Without question many study abroad programs came into being simply because energetic faculty members hustled to make them happen. In some cases the faculty motives were entirely pure and altruistic; that is, to advance one or more of the educational objectives described above. But in many cases also the objectives were more selfish and personal, including development of a means to gain summer or other salary supplements (academic "piecework," as some called it), a trip overseas, access to research opportunities abroad, or a chance to proselytize majors for a department that needed them. Typically where generous sabbatical leave opportunities and travel funds are available at an institution, and where salary and promotion decisions are based above all on research and publication, the incentives for faculty entrepreneurship in study abroad are much reduced. Whether a positive institutional response to aggressive entrepreneurial behavior of this kind is a good thing cannot be answered here. That a cooperative institutional response to those initiatives of entrepreneurial faculty is in fact one of the most prominent goals behind many programs can, however, be recognized clearly.

14. Sell the kids what they want

One perspective on study abroad is that, like the cafeteria or movie theater, its educational significance is minimal. However, the student customers want it and, therefore, the institution should perform some kind of market research and deliver an attractive product at a price that the market will bear. Because of the seemingly crass and unflattering sound this goal has to academic ears it is often camouflaged and seldom expressed as boldly as it is here. However, it was plain that the perception of study abroad as a consumer good did prevail in some of the institutions we visited. One indication that this goal, rather than another, is indeed being pursued by an institution may be the placement of study abroad programs in some nonacademic part of the institution, or in a remote corner of academic affairs.

15. Give them a break

Many of America's most successful and attractive liberal arts colleges are located in rural environments or small towns. Whether by design, or not, study abroad has come to provide for some students an extremely popular interlude in the four years of education offered by these schools. In part the option of "getting away" increases the applicant pool; but in part also the safety valve provided by the junior year away responds to those who get "stir crazy" and cuts down on the number of transfers outward. Many of these colleges recognize the problem openly and work hard to cope with it. In particular they seek to develop junior-year experiences, both at home and abroad, that will be educationally valuable and will return the students to the home campus invigorated and refreshed for their senior year.

Some with whom we talked went even further than this diagnosis. They argued that today the four-year, liberal arts, undergraduate degree program is an anachronism: It is simply too long and the students recognize this instinctively in their "sophomore slump." The junior year or semester abroad is one way for the students to deal with this deeper problem. The problem is more intense in the rural liberal arts college simply because students in metropolitan areas more easily find other ways to vent their frustration.

16. *Give employers and admissions officers what they want*

We heard conflicting testimony about whether the recent rise in popularity of study abroad is a response to real or perceived pressures from employers for more cosmopolitan employees. Most observers concede that the rhetoric of chief executive officers could lead one easily to that conclusion. But some, at least, say that this view has not visibly filtered down to the recruiting officers. Others report anecdotally how employers respond favorably to foreign experiences not only because of the presumed language skills that they need but because of the initiative and adventurous spirit they imply. Deans of professional schools testified confidently that study abroad had affected their own admissions decisions (a year at the London School of Economics "wows them" in law or business), particularly in marginal cases and where an interview gives the applicant an opportunity to wax eloquent about what it meant. Only a few persons suggested that study abroad might be a negative factor in employment, this when a particular experience is perceived as frivolous. There was near unanimity that serious study in such "remote" countries as Japan and the Soviet Union was especially attractive to employers.

Whether or not study abroad has these positive career implications it is interesting to see the advocates claim that it does. The following extract is from the Freshman Advising Manual at one of the colleges we visited.

To be liberally educated has always required knowledge and sensitivity transcending the limits of one's own culture, but now in a world that is increasingly economically and politically interdependent, cross-cultural understanding is as much a practical necessity as an educational ideal. For just those reasons, study abroad is a sign of the initiative and breadth

often looked for by medical, law and other professional
schools, and by employers.

17. *Make or save money*

A force impelling the growth of study abroad in recent years has
undoubtedly been the wish or expectation of one or more participants in the process to "make a buck." Economic conditions differ
widely among different kinds of institutions, big and small, public
and private, popular and unpopular. Therefore the opportunity to
make a profit varies widely. Few educational institutions are
shrewd enough to know for certain what their revenues and costs
truly are. Nevertheless some institutions do believe that they can
"make" money on study abroad, and from their testimony it is
plausible that they do. Conditions necessary for an institutionally
profitable operation include, in economists' terms, high marginal
revenue and low marginal cost. High marginal revenue may mean
both high fees charged to students going abroad and high tuition
charged to additional students admitted on the home campus to
fill the places of the departed. Typically only residential private
universities in great demand among high school seniors find high
marginal revenue a certainty. If a "hot" undergraduate college
with fixed dormitory space and limited campus common facilities
is able to add to its on-campus student body a cohort of extra
students equal to those who go abroad, the total payments received
from those overseas are net revenue. Administrators at one major
private university confessed to us candidly that they encouraged
study abroad mainly because they were desperately short of beds
on campus; in fact they had substantially more promises than beds.
By filling the class spaces left open by student departures overseas
with transfer students admitted on condition they would not have
campus beds, the bed shortage was solved and the cost of constructing or leasing a new dormitory saved. Administrators at a
major public university told us of a similar practice, but they confessed to anxiety over the consequences if the study abroad students had suddenly to return home. They said they felt like the
man in the half-ton truck carrying a ton of canaries: He had to

keep banging the side of the truck to keep the canaries in the air – if they ever came to roost at once, he would be in big trouble.

Marginal cost will be determined in part by the extent to which it is necessary to engage new resources (people and equipment) to operate the overseas programs. If it is possible to use tenured faculty who would not otherwise have been fully utilized, or if teachers and facilities can be engaged inexpensively overseas, then marginal costs may be kept low. Private institutions, unfettered by rules and regulations of state legislatures, bureaucracies, and system administrations, are likely to be more effective than public institutions at keeping real marginal costs to a minimum. For these reasons it is not surprising to find private colleges and universities among the most energetic merchandisers of study abroad.

One exception to this generalization about the comparative aggressiveness of private schools is the public institution that concludes that, through the attractiveness of study abroad, it may increase its enrollments, upon which its public subventions are fixed. It is difficult to be certain if this enrollment goal was actually pursued in any of the institutions we visited, but it was said to be so in several of the public colleges.

However it is not only institutions that may profit from study abroad. Depending upon fee structures, and provisions for transfer of certain credits, many students have enjoyed a period of study abroad at lower net cost than if they had stayed at home. For students the most financially advantageous situation we encountered was the following: A liberal arts college with very high tuition permitted students in their junior year to enroll in low-cost programs operated by other schools and allowed full transfer of credits back to the college with no payment of local tuition. In one college the rapid acceleration in junior-year departures that these conditions precipitated required a sudden and drastic change in the rules.

Still a third group able to make money from study abroad is the plethora of intermediate extramural institutions that either operate study abroad programs for students of several colleges and universities or else provide services of many kinds to such students. "Profit" is not technically the term to describe the results of these efforts because most are formally "not-for-profit." However their financial success in recent years has been demonstrated by their healthy survival and growth in numbers. It remains to be seen whether the strong dollar was crucial to this success and whether the growth will survive the recent dollar weakness.

One grizzled veteran of decades of work with study abroad told us in no uncertain terms that there is no money to be made there, that there is no room for academic entrepreneurs in this business – and that we should tell our readers so. We conclude that, indeed, from a commercial perspective study abroad is a highly risky endeavor. But at the same time it has in the past paid off for some, and there seems little doubt that financial reward will remain a goal of some of those who pursue it in future.

18. Interinstitutional linkages

At least some overseas study has been initiated by faculty and administrators as a device to establish the basis for more extensive international interinstitutional cooperation of various kinds. Often the development of links is solicited by a foreign unit, varying from an academic department to a foreign ministry. The ultimate objective of the overture may be a multifaceted exchange of faculty and other personnel, but the easiest point at which to initiate the process is an exchange of students. Typically interinstitutional charges for this purpose are of modest size.

An excellent example of interinstitutional links that have paid off is at the University of Massachusetts, where a relationship with the universities of Baden–Württemberg has blossomed from student exchanges into faculty exchanges, joint research, and "institutional bonding" in various forms. Many current linkages between institutions are merely statements formalized with signatures and seals. The opportunity for development of truly beneficial relationships, however, remains largely unexplored.

19. Response to governmental policy

Some individual study abroad has in the past been inspired and supported by government projects – notably the Fulbright Program and to a lesser degree AID for research at the graduate level. We sensed that colleges and universities are sensitive still to Federal and state governmental priorities and believe that those students who are prepared will benefit from new funds made available. We were struck, for example, by the sensitive resonance we detected in Texas to potential opportunities under President Reagan's Caribbean Basin Initiative. Similarly in California, Governor Deukmejian's focus on the Pacific Rim has captivated not only the public but private colleges as well. Increasingly, foreign governments are providing stimulus for developments in study abroad. The German government, in particular, has been active for years under the Deutscher Akademischer Austauschdienst (DAAD). But others have been involved as well, notably the Japanese, who see the presence of American students and faculty in their midst as one way of encouraging reform of their own university system.

Institutional renewal

American higher education, by and large, is ill equipped to deal with institutional obsolescence, lassitude, and overall degradation. Budgets have few openings to promote innovation. Tenure removes many of the incentives for responsiveness from those who have it, and excludes from the action those who do not. Most of the stimuli for change within higher education have been external: wars, land grant legislation, foreign policy offensives, cold war fears about science and technology, and so on. Leaders of a few institutions have seen the new social drive for study abroad in the 1980s as one more external force that might, if correctly channeled, have this larger but indirect result. In consequence they view the movement of faculty and administrators abroad as an extremely valuable byproduct of the process. Thereby the curriculum and the research output can be reformed and confronted with the world. Clearly this particular goal must be discussed on a campus with great delicacy if at all; but we found both that it was uppermost in the minds of some articulate exponents of foreign study and, from our conversations with participants, that it had indeed had some of the intended results.

Beyond the macro objective of broad institutional regeneration there is the opportunity for the rehabilitation of an individual faculty member through participation in study abroad. This can be achieved either through a redirection of teaching or through access to research materials. This potential contribution of overseas study programs should gladden the hearts and ensure the cooperation of those hard-pressed deans and department chairpersons who wrestle regularly with faculty deterioration. Program directors would do well to explore and exploit this opportunity to the full.

A plethora of goals – a paucity of instruments

There are virtually an unlimited number of valuable endeavors that can engage a student during an educational career on any campus. However, the curriculum and the hours in the day are finite. Any new activity must necessarily squeeze out an old one. An economist would point out that the price of the new is the "opportunity cost" involved in loss of the old. We are quite aware that those who call for more study abroad to be added to a degree program must be prepared for something else to be removed. The opportunity cost of novelty is especially visible in highly structured programs like those in technical, scientific, and professional areas. Study abroad may mean missing Biology 165 or Fluid Mechanics 297. Therefore it is especially important to spell out clearly for these cases what will be gained by the exchange. A list of goals and potential accomplishments in overseas study such as the one we have provided here is a good point at which to begin this demonstration. A list of this kind does not prove results of study abroad but it does at least suggest potential contributions.

Trade-offs must be faced by an institution as well as by students, but the constraints there are different. For the institution as a whole activities can be increased so long as resources for their support can be found. The essential institutional task is to relate ends responsibly to means. It is a well-known maxim of the theory of public policy that to formulate an effective strategy the number of available policy instruments must be at least as great as the number of goals. For example, you can aim for both price stability and full employment if you have access to both monetary and fiscal policy. You may not always achieve the desired results but you can at least aim monetary policy at the price level and fiscal policy at job creation. If you have only monetary policy to do both jobs, you will be faced inevitably with wrenching trade-offs and compromises. Contraction of the money supply may restrain prices but cut jobs at the same time. The same principles apply in university administration.

For study abroad we have identified nineteen discrete goals, some of which might plausibly be achieved by a single multifaceted program instrument but many of which are philosophically and administratively in conflict with one another and cannot be sought together. Two approaches can be taken to this seeming dilemma: Instruments (programs) can be increased or goals can be reduced. In fact, most institutions do both, although without consciously realizing it. Most colleges and universities offer a range of study abroad options to their students, with various goals in view. They run their own programs and they make available the programs of others. At the same time they give priority to certain study abroad objectives over others.

One way in which the responsibility for pursuing many goals at one time can be handled effectively is by allocating tasks among the different layers of authority. Typically goals 1–5 may be perceived as institutionwide, and therefore the responsibility for them may be expected to fall on the central administration. Goals 6–9 are the natural concern of departments, schools, and their individual faculty members. Goals 10–18 and institutional renewal are usually shared among the three layers of campus governance (central, departmental, and individual), requiring some coordination to avoid duplication and waste of effort. Some academic administrators in a misplaced fit of neatness propose reducing drastically a plethora of study abroad programs that seem, on the surface, to be aimed at the same goal – to get Johnny to Paris – whereas in reality these many programs may be the best way to achieve the substantial range of benefits that can come from study abroad. We urge that before administrators perform triage they look carefully at the diverse goals of these programs; they may find that the many separately programmable instruments they have in place are all needed to meet the surprisingly abundant objectives that are well within their institutional reach.

3

Ways to do it

The aquatic alternatives

The hundreds of programs for study abroad at American colleges and universities represent almost an infinity of models of how it can be done. In order to understand the range of choice open to an institution contemplating a new or modified program it is useful to divide models roughly into categories that constitute segments of a continuum. Those who operate or observe study abroad programs often justify or condemn the other alternatives in most passionate terms. The advocates of one model speak scornfully of others and ecstatically of their own. Conflicts between contending positions occasionally reach high peaks of emotion. It appears that both adherence to principle and the conflicting self-interests of the contenders help to explain this characteristic tension. It may be that our own lack of involvement in any particular type of program deprives us of both passion and strong conviction on the subject. We can see merit as well as problems in most models and positions. As a result we present here the alternatives together with those arguments, for and against, that we judge to have some potential validity. The identification of strength or weakness in each case will depend to some extent upon one's own particular values and assessment of local circumstances.

Discussion of study abroad is conducted often through metaphors of various kinds, including especially those from athletics, evolutionary theory, and several other areas. One of the most popular pictures students overseas facing a river of foreign higher education and having to decide how to enter it and whether to move with the current. We invoke this metaphor to differentiate among the several distinct institutional approaches to study abroad.

Total immersion: plunging into midstream

Perhaps the most strongly held position by some in the field of international education is that study abroad is an experience to be reserved for the strongest, the fittest, and the best prepared. It must be a privilege to be earned and an accomplishment to be won over high odds. It is almost like an initiation rite. In the most extreme version this model specifies that students of exceptional ability shall be identified for study abroad early in their careers – in their freshman year or even before if possible. They must be educated thoroughly in the language and culture of the country to which they will go (or else their experience will be simply a vacation). They must be put through a rigorous application process, including ideally an interview and an essay, and then sent to the foreign country to take a full course load for a full academic year at a high-quality indigenous institution, therein to cope with all the problems that native students must face, plus the special ones that foreign students bring with them. The analogy used to illustrate this model is of an American institution picking a very small number of willing and potentially superlative swimmers (almost like an Olympic team), training them thoroughly in the aquatic arts, and then throwing them, arms and legs flailing, into the midstream of foreign higher education. A few may simply sink beneath the waves, others may scream for rescue, but most, if they have been well selected and prepared, will catch the rhythm of the stream quickly, compete successfully with the locals, and emerge immensely invigorated from the experience – credit to their teachers, to their country, and to themselves. Special treatment or coaching while in the foreign waters, almost like cheating on exams, would be counterproductive and would detract from the value of the experience. Virtually by definition the American institution should not worry about the quality of the education the "immersed" student receives, except that it be the best the foreign country can offer. An authentic experience is the goal. Nor should the American institution attempt to make the host institution mend any of its ways. No American college or university can or should expect to have a significant impact on a foreign institution to which it is contributing but a few visiting students.

Provision for transfer back home of equivalent course work may be arranged ad hoc in this model on the understanding that it is the student's responsibility to make a convincing case to the home authorities.

This model of study abroad and variants of it are defended with almost religious zeal by its supporters, who are mainly faculty members and study abroad directors at the institutions of origin. Its most enthusiastic advocates are found especially in prestigious highly selective colleges and universities. On our travels we heard especially forceful defenses of this model at the University of Texas at Austin. We listened hard to try to understand why these and other spokespersons felt so strongly. We suggest four reasons.

First, some faculty argue that weaker and less well prepared students simply cannot benefit from an educational experience overseas – from tourism perhaps, but not from a serious intellectual challenge. Unless students can "engage fully" a foreign culture through access to the language, higher education, and an understanding of their surroundings, they will not be able to comprehend what they see. Their time would be better spent at home, and in the worst case they may return from a foreign sojourn with less appreciation, rather than more, for what they have seen and with their prejudices merely strengthened by their inability to test them against reality. In terms of social theory the total immersion advocates hold to a belief that "participant observation" is in this area the only road to truth. External observers can never really understand what they see.

Second, some American faculty see study abroad participants as "cultural ambassadors" and unofficial representatives of American higher education; hence we must send only the very best. Scholars abroad will judge us, as well as our students, by their capacity to perform. Therefore we should let them see only our star performers. The rest of the world will assume that we will send abroad only our finest, and if we do not our reputation will suffer grievously by our average being mistaken for our best. One variant of this argument is that American academe has a responsibility to protect the rest of the world from its worst students!

Third, it seems clear in discussions with the more zealous advocates of this approach (often characterized as "mainstreaming") that the familiar academic "Pygmalion complex" helps to explain the level of enthusiasm senior scholars have for first-class, dedicated, hard-working junior scholars. They see in these young people either what they themselves were in their youth, what they remember themselves to have been, what they wish they had been, or what they believe now they ought to have been. The vision of the binational and bilingual, or even multinational and multilingual, young scholar moving easily around the globe among different cultures and linguistic groups presents a model that is supremely gratifying and satisfying to the academic mind, and especially to those with an ascetic bent who recognize the enormous labor this style presupposes.

Finally, we sense that many American faculty in selective institutions recoil instinctively at the mass higher education of which they are a privileged part. They neither enjoy nor can defend in principle spending much of their time with less able or less motivated students. Their hearts go out to the intellectual cream. They recoil at the skimmed milk. Faculty at both private and public institutions rail at athletes, alumni children, "special admits" of various kinds, and other students who draw down the scholarly average and the intellectual atmosphere of their classes. They recognize that such lesser persons will probably continue to gain entry to their classes, but they do not like it. In planning for and operating study abroad programs these faculty are, as it were, given a window on utopia. Unconstrained apparently by the wishes and regulations of legislators, trustees, and other external forces, they can construct and argue for, in this small microcosm of higher education, the limitation and restriction that they would secretly love to impose throughout the educational system. They desire, perhaps subconsciously, to limit higher education to the intellectual élite – "those who can make good use of it." So they propose to demand a 3.2 GPA, language fluency, and a willingness to sacrifice. They also propose various other barriers designed to prevent the inferior, or even the merely average, student from taking part.

We have described here the most pure form of rigorous mainstreaming. There are also adulterated forms that still fall within the category. The irreducible core elements of mainstreaming are full participation in an indigenous foreign university and use of the foreign language. Some programs preserve these elements but will facilitate the transfer of credit, encourage living with a sympathetic local family, provide the services of an advisor and a preparatory language program, tolerate a shorter period of foreign residence than a full year, and in other ways cushion the process without changing the character of it fundamentally. The University of California System "Education Overseas Program" qualifies in this respect. The Rhodes and Marshall scholarships are for mainstreamers, as are the DAAD scholarships provided by the German government.

The critics of this model find that its faults grow directly out of its virtues. In particular they complain that the rigor and restrictive requirements (especially mastery of a foreign language) limit it to a very few – mostly language and area studies majors. They object to the very élitist character of the program that makes it so attractive to its proponents. Moreover, the critics say, many American students underestimate language problems, and they will be overwhelmed by mainstreaming. They claim also that the theoretical base of the program is fundamentally flawed: There is no evidence in the social sciences that participant observation is indeed an especially effective pedagogical or analytical technique. Furthermore, they say, the objective of foreign study should be not to create a bicultural person, able to reflect the culture of another nation as well as his/her own, but rather to form a truly transnational student able critically to assess the cultures of all nations.

Finally, the critics point out that almost all systems of higher education around the world have too many structural differences from the American system to make widespread direct exchanges practicable. Not only are there often no equivalents to college life, personal advising, required class attendance, and regular tests and

examinations but the basic notion of cumulative course credit leading to a degree does not exist. Accordingly the problem of determining equivalence and transfer credit can be very great. Most
higher education elsewhere in the world, moreover, is more heavily
subsidized in proportion to total costs than in the United States.
Tuition is usually minimal or nonexistent. Mainstreaming of large
numbers of American students abroad, therefore, could involve
the significant sharing by foreigners in this provision of a public
service, a condition not likely to be tolerated for long by foreign
voters and taxpayers.

Swimming in the eddies

A second approach to study abroad amounts to a far less strenuous
immersion in a foreign educational system, for briefer periods and
under conditions that safeguard life and limb. The students in this
model are encouraged to swim and flex their muscles, but not too
vigorously and under close supervision of a lifeguard with ready
access to a life preserver. The fundamental presumption of this
model as it was explained to us is that an educational experience
abroad is "civilizing and liberating." Consequently for most students "the ramp should not be too steep." There are several characteristic forms of this approach that can be reviewed.

The first variant is to place American students in "schools for
foreigners" abroad, which are freestanding (and even sometimes
profit-making) institutions connected or not with a local university
but operated with the special problems of non–native speakers in
mind. These schools vary in their rigor, but they exist to serve a
different clientele from the native students. Their focus is principally on the local language and culture, and they may specialize
in an intensive program intended to produce workable fluency in
a few months. The student body is multinational, and American
students encounter a cosmopolitan community to supplement their
exposure to the new culture in which the school is embedded.
Sometimes students in a school for foreigners take one or more
courses at a local university at the same time as they study at the
school, but the emphasis is upon careful and limited challenges to

those students who now find themselves in an unfamiliar environment. Typically the staff and administration of the school are unusually sensitive to the needs of their foreign charges and will not often require of them 100 meter freestyle intellectual sprints. A variety of living facilities may be available, ranging from sympathetic local families to an international dormitory.

A second device to assist and protect the less adventuresome student abroad under this model is a "resident advisor" from the home college or university living nearby and charged to watch closely over the student's welfare. Not only is the student abroad under this model kept out of the mainstream; he is provided with a swimming coach. Responsibilities of the advisor may include academic and personal counseling, negotiation for living facilities (unlike the mainstreamers who have to fend for themselves to arrange living accommodations), some modest instruction and tutoring, intervention with the local instructors, and interpretation of both local curriculum and grading for transfer home. In some cases these advisors are American faculty on short– or long-term leave; in other cases they are indigenous persons engaged full- or part-time for the purpose. Depending upon the program, and especially the affluence of the sponsoring institution, advisors may have responsibility for American students at a single foreign institution, at all the institutions in a city or country, or even for all the students in a region or continent. Some maintain twenty-four-hour "hot lines" (usually manned by faculty from the American institution who spend at least one academic year abroad working with the overseas program) for instant communication of crises by their charges. Some institutions we visited sent out advisors from the United States at intervals, rather like circuit-riding clergymen. Others, with greater financial constraints, attempted to perform some of the advisory functions by international communication.

One of the side benefits of this variant may be that U.S. graduate students, otherwise excluded from overseas experience, are brought along as teaching assistants. A function the graduate students can perform, if well selected, is to serve as a bridge between the undergraduates and the surrounding community. Dangers facing programs in this category, and in the one that follows, will always be their artificiality and isolation. Steps being taken by programs that recognize this danger include location in a large metropolis rather than small towns, and placement of students in local homes rather than in central dormitories.

In these variants of study abroad academic credit is effortlessly assured to participating students, either by prearranged transfer of equivalent units or by direct registration in the home institution's courses. Sometimes the credit students in these programs receive is designated "study abroad" and sometimes not.

Faculty of American institutions vary widely in their appraisals of programs in this second category. If they themselves have taken part, they are likely to be positive. If not, they will probably concede grudgingly that this structure is desirable because of the lack of preparation and unwillingness of most American students to undertake the rigors of the mainstream. The essence of this criticism has been expressed nicely in a recent speech by Dr. Joe Neal, for many years Director, Office of International Programs at the University of Texas at Austin. He reported:

> I seem to see a movement away from the linguistically prepared, academically trained, and carefully selected individual who goes overseas to study in the curriculum and language of the host institution in competition with the student's peers in the local nation.
>
> Instead, the movement seems to be toward groups of students selected primarily on the basis of economic ability rather than grade-point average and carefully guarded and shepherded by babysitters who provide services from September until May guaranteeing a safe return to the arms of airport-waiting families at the conclusion of the year abroad.
>
> Often these groups of students, carefully compiled in order to provide complimentary transportation for the babysitter, are taught by this person overseas in a classroom. There they sit listening to the same language they could have heard on their own campus, learning from the same textbooks, the identical lecture notes that were brought over in worn suit-

cases, and periodically they look outside their glass windows and there they see a foreign country.

For this privilege they pay not only their university tuition but a surcharge which covers the cost of travel and the housing and often the dependents of the babysitter as well as an additional surcharge for the local firm, often American in origin, which has arranged rental for the room in which they sit as well as connections with local travel agencies who haul them about the country on planned tours.

I have discussed this subject at length with good friends who are involved in this business. Normally the babysitters come back exhausted and worn because of the hazardous duty to which they have been exposed. The entrepreneurs defend their participation. Their argument runs like this. The majority of American students are linguistically ignorant, uninformed on the history and politics of other nations, culturally inept, and unable to go abroad at all except under the conditions described above. Granted that they do not receive an education in its whole term but at least half an education is better than none, and so is the apathy and indifference of our campus scholastic populations that even this device is constructive in its total impact.

Generally faculty lean toward making these programs in the eddies more demanding, rather than less, and will nudge them out into the currents. Faculty in the humanities in particular profess some embarrassment at the need for such devices and will sometimes press for more prerequisites, such as language fluency.

We sensed that in general the climate is moving against this style of study abroad, just as it seems to be moving against unstructured general education of all kinds. Faculty on campuses even where this style is well-planned and well-conducted feel a certain embarrassment about it.

In almost all cases swimming in the eddies requires a substantially greater financial investment than does mainstreaming. We were told on several campuses that this condition had profound institutional implications. If an institution has purchased or leased space and employed people at substantial cost, its leeway to pursue academic rigor or tight quality control may be constrained. As one program director put it, the specter of "the empty-bed syndrome" is always before you. The negative effects of this constraint are being felt more and more as economic pressures mount.

Staying by the pool

An extreme variant of swimming in the eddies involves the construction of a special facility abroad to permit only very occasional and selective immersion in the river of foreign higher education. In this case the home institution sets up a special program, sometimes termed pejoratively an "enclave," using predominantly local staff and reflecting only to a very limited extent the curriculum and teaching methods of the host country. Such programs are designed to expose American students to the foreign system of higher education only from afar, under controlled conditions, and with ultimate responsibility for quality and content resting with the home institution. Indeed the higher education of the country visited is of secondary interest. The primary focus of these programs is upon the culture and artifacts of the region where they are located, perused from the stance of an appreciative observer.

The purest form of the enclave model is the self-contained teaching and living centers operated for decades by Stanford University across Western Europe. These "overseas campuses," located usually in rural areas, are designed to provide easy access to local folkways, away from the hectic pace of the cosmopolitan cities. The centers are also comfortable bases for expeditions to places of high culture throughout the region. The curriculum is mainly at the introductory level and oriented toward the culture and society of the Western European country where the center is placed. One academic quarter is the typical time period for a Stanford period abroad and language requirements are minimal. The informal motto is "no hassle, no language." Originally only Stanford faculty taught in the overseas centers, but native instructors have gradually grown in number. Special emphasis is given to highly personalized education, and the growth of community among the relatively small group of faculty and students is considered an important by-product of the experience.

But even Stanford has become increasingly uneasy with this longstanding and celebrated model. A recent report by a faculty committee suggests: "In essence the enclave centers became worlds unto themselves – always isolated from Europe and increasingly cut off from the direction of education at home." Moreover:

> there is a discontinuity between academic offerings abroad and the programs they are following at home. This discontinuity has heightened the sense that there exists a distinct and expensive trade-off between doing more introductory work overseas and continuing to deepen specialized knowledge at Stanford ... Many of Stanford's academically advanced and most interesting students are not able to spend a period abroad. Because they are committed to serious development of deeply held intellectual interests, the current concentration of disaggregated and introductory level courses overseas does not outweigh their opportunities at home ... The ephemeral nature of such disintegrated programs which neither constitute a progression from earlier work nor a foundation for planned further study renders the period overseas for many a kind of time out from the pressures of a Stanford education. ... Most importantly, academic discontinuity is unacceptable because it abandons the enormous potential educational advantages that would accompany an integrated program enriching a wide range of Stanford curricula by adding a complementary understanding of their increasing international dimensions.

In 1986 Stanford was exploring alternative new approaches to overseas study. Its goal is to make overseas programs as challenging and stimulating as any on the home campus. To symbolize their intent to interact more with the indigenous scholarly community the center in the United Kingdom has been moved from Cliveden, the magnificent Astor estate, to a building on the Oxford High Street. There are plans also to move outward from the traditional concentration on Western Europe to the "periphery" in the Third World.

Paddling in the shallows

Programs in this fourth category make relatively little use of the local environment of the countries in which they are located. There are two kinds. First, there are programs established within foreign countries by American colleges and universities as extensions of their local campuses. In varying degrees these programs maintain isolation from their environment and, it is argued, they retain quality control by teaching their normal curriculum with regular faculty in a special facility bought, built, or leased for the purpose. Students usually live together in a special dormitory and are shepherded about in groups. The benefits of this category are said to be almost entirely atmospheric, and prior preparation by students need be only minimal. Although like the Stanford centers in structure, these programs do not make a conscious effort to engage the local culture. They are just there.

The second form in this fourth category is the "study tour" made up of intersemester special projects, summer sojourns, and other forms of flying visits to a foreign area for which very limited or no preparation is required. Several liberal arts and community colleges we visited were especially imaginative in putting these together, calling them sometimes "nontraditional instruction." Often they grew out of home-institution courses for which another country provides the laboratory, especially in such fields as art history, archeology, foreign area studies, architecture, and geology. But there are also examples of short courses in law, business, education, engineering and other applied fields, as there are in "backpacking" and "reef diving."

As a group, faculty members are most dubious about this category of study abroad. They accuse their brethren who conduct such programs of doing so for personal gain and they charge them with prostituting themselves and their craft. They use a variety of pejorative terms to describe the process, such as bubble, birdhouse, and day-care for adults. In this category especially we may discern in faculty attitudes a reflection of views toward larger issues of higher education as much as toward study abroad. In expressing themselves on this narrower question, they are spared the political ramifications inside and outside their institutions of making charges on larger issues. In this case their criticism seems to be mainly toward the extension of higher education to "the masses," and its shading in the community college into technical, remedial, adult, and even secondary education. Projects in this category are the antithesis of those élite programs in the first category. They encompass courses on cooking in Paris and camping in Canada. Clearly some of the programs offered to "paddlers in shallows" do trail off almost indistinguishably into simple tourism, and their potential tax deductibility to users seems often to be as significant as their educational value. (For example, we were informed that a summer course for physicians on health programs in the United Kingdom, offered by a community college, was especially popular.)

Paradoxically, because of the bad scholarly odor in which programs in this category are held, they do not receive very much careful and sympathetic attention from leaders in the academic world. The director of one such program said that he and his students felt very much as step-children. The result of this nose-in-the-air attitude is that correctable problems in these programs frequently do not get handled and the very considerable opportunities for constructive contribution that they yield are not recognized and exploited. Large-enrollment public institutions, in particular, need guidance on such questions as whether part-time faculty should be allowed to participate, whether resources can legitimately be diverted from other activities for these programs, what "standards" are appropriate, and whether programs should be instituted for a special purpose such as a local firm's proposed overseas marketing thrust (e.g., a course entitled "Let's Learn about Asia"). Such institutions need all the help they can get in determining the legitimacy and designing the details of such programs.

Wind sprints to the raft

In contrast to the first four categories of study abroad this form involves entering the river relatively briefly, but vigorously and designedly. Whereas students taking part in the categories of study abroad examined to this point have aimed to benefit from the wide experience of bathing, whether more or less energetically, and the medium is the message, so to speak, students in this category have a narrow focus and specific purposes in their exercise. They go not for some generalized experiential benefit but on a particular mission. They go for an archeological dig, as student teachers required to gain exposure to an unfamiliar culture, as business students exploring foreign corporations, or as art history majors gaining acquaintance with the essential subject matter of their field. Participants in programs of this kind will typically venture forth as the wards, as it were, of one specialized faculty member. They will have their eyes trained clearly on their objective and may, or may not, be connected to the more generalized study abroad program at their institutions.

One of the attractive features of these wind sprints is that they can often be fitted into the nooks and crannies of the academic year, thereby not detracting either from the work of the regular term or from employment in the summer. If their form and content are too unusual, moreover, they can be offered by Continuing Education. Construction of this kind of study abroad usually requires imagination and a willingness overall to bend the rules. This is clearly the rubric through which certain frequently underrepresented groups can be served. For example, we encountered at the University of Southern California a short summer program in Cambridge on Victorian England for older students pursuing the Master of Liberal Studies degree.

Row your own boat

A category of study abroad that seems to be growing rapidly in size, variety, and popularity is the work experience, "internship," or "externship," as it is sometimes called. In this form the American student does not even enter the river of foreign higher education but instead rides above it, as it were, in a rowboat of special employment. By participating directly in the culture that is of interest the student is placed in intimate contact with its facts and circumstances. Social service becomes a route to cultural learning. The home college or university may explicitly provide the analytical constructs wherewith to understand what is experienced by the intern, or it is sometimes assumed that the educational process does this automatically. We encountered a wide variety of styles of internship. Some are conducted during the academic year, others during the summer; some are unstructured, others require a student to keep a log and prepare a paper; some are combined with course work, others stand alone; some bring credit to the student, others do not. Internships seem to respond to the wants of many of today's students. They are consistent in some cases with a careerist orientation, in others with a wish to contribute even before entering the regular job market. For some they provide a welcome break from the intense pressures of undergraduate study at certain colleges. In cases where they do not yield course credit and are offered during the summer they meet the wishes of some faculty for a foreign experience for their students that does not "water down" the prescribed curriculum. Internships have been arranged in a wide variety of places: in U.S. government offices overseas, international organizations, doctors' and lawyers' offices, newspapers, manufacturing firms, local government offices, and legislatures. Usually they provide no remuneration and therefore afford no problems of work permits and taxation. Sometimes colleges and universities send their own representatives to negotiate internships directly; in others they engage local "placehunters." Harvard University for its Ventures Abroad Program makes use of a network of 1,357 alumni advisors in seventy-four countries to generate short-term employment and internships overseas. Some of these, it is true, are in the foreign branches of American firms, or in multinationals; but even there the testimony we encountered was widely enthusiastic. At Boston University we heard that one of the most valuable experiences of an internship came in facing, understanding, and coping with anti-American sentiment overseas.

A Tufts intern in Madrid became a popular radio announcer known as "The Girl from Boston."

Internships, especially when offered out of term, are one relatively painless way of introducing study abroad to students from fields that hitherto have stood aloof. We were impressed to find many internship programs that extended well beyond undergraduate and graduate programs in the arts and sciences into professional areas of engineering, medicine, law, journalism, architecture, and public policy. These are offered by foreign sponsors as well as by American institutions. A program begun in the 1980s by the Bosch Foundation in Germany is epecially noteworthy.

Initially internships were limited mainly to Western Europe, but we ran across an impressive number of instances where recently they have been extended to the newly industrialized countries (Korea, Taiwan, Hong Kong, etc.), to Japan, and even to Eastern Europe, China, and the Third World, where the style is reminiscent of the Peace Corps.

Room for a thousand bathers

The categories of kinds of study abroad outlined here blur easily into each other at the edges. Moreover, the selection to date by institutions from among these categories does not follow tightly any institutional characteristics (e.g., size, rigor, prestige, difficulty of entry, public/private, complexity of makeup). The accidents of history and personality, rather than any kind of visible logic, seem most important in explaining the contemporary landscape of study abroad.

Typically the preponderance of views among those with whom we spoke at any given institution was overwhelmingly in favor of only one of these, even though several might grudgingly be tolerated. It is customary to express scorn and derision for the others. We ourselves were left, however, with the sense that these models need not be in conflict, nor indeed is it necessary to select among them. We reached an Aristotelian position that there may be good and bad forms in each category and that American higher education can afford to have swimmers all over the river, benefiting from all locations and aquatic styles and without necessarily injuring or even splashing the others. We believe that the most beneficial posture for any enlightened institution is an open mind and eclectic approach shaped by the strengths and disposition of that particular institution.

Several of the institutions we visited have built up over the years highly skilled and sophisticated study abroad officers able to support and assist swimmers in many modes. They advise and inform the mainstreamers. They support and sustain those in the eddies. They provide the logistics for paddlers, swimmers to the raft, oarsmen, and in some cases, sitters by the pool. They are careful not to be too judgmental about particular modes but count upon their campus community to move in the directions that currently make most sense. We are persuaded this is the best way for any institution to proceed.

Several universities were deep in ferment about study abroad and were yielding, we think, remarkably fresh and innovative ideas about how to approach it. To return to Stanford once again, a proposal there is to redirect their efforts fundamentally from isolated enclaves to effective "cross-fertilization" with institutions abroad through "sustained joint academic interaction." They will search for "ways of increasing programmatic reciprocity and diminishing the sense of quasi-parasitism that characterizes American education abroad." The proposal at Stanford is to integrate overseas study far more closely with other programs on campus and to adopt any modes that will accomplish this goal. The faculty report recommends that Stanford:

> ... build upon its recognized strengths in innovative interdisciplinary fields and its unique position in the emerging global order to create a network of centers that function jointly on a multinational scale. In addition to their established role of general liberal cultivation, overseas centers should elaborate more specialized teaching and research concentrations closely integrated with important curricula and cross-disciplinary programs at Stanford and operate interactively with cooperative institutions abroad. These programs

should examine the contemporary development of the international system, the relation between technology and political and social organization in advanced industrial societies,
and the uncertain evolution in the coming period of tension
between national and transnational cultures.

This posture of flexibility and openness to different ways of conducting overseas study appropriate for ever-changing objectives of
the academic community seems the most sensible approach for
institutions today.

4

Tasks to be done

In many respects study abroad constitutes a microcosm of the institution of which it is a part. The functions to be performed in connection with study abroad are simply those that must be undertaken to operate the institution as a whole. If the study abroad program of another college or university, a national organization, a cooperative body, or a commercial provider is used, then the performance of some of these functions may be avoided. There is a danger, however, of assuming that because the administration of study abroad often occurs in a small office outside the main academic structure it can be done easily, casually, by following some simple agreed-upon formula, or even neglected.

In this chapter we review the tasks that are typically associated with study abroad. Some are tasks that fall naturally to the faculty and some are the responsibility of the administration. We think there is advantage in facing these tasks squarely. It is true that, because of the nature of higher education, if tasks are not recognized clearly, there is still some provision for muddling through; but in this event there is bound to be a cost in efficiency.

This is not by any means a complete list of tasks related to study abroad, but it is a good start and should warn the newcomer and remind the old-timer what lies ahead.

Tasks for the faculty and department

1. Establish and approve curriculum

Alternative models for constructing and approving study abroad curricula involve leaving this to one of the following:

(a) an independent study abroad office that knows the constraints under which the curriculum will be offered and what will sell, but may not have the confidence of the faculty;

(b) the relevant academic departments which may act like lobbies;

(c) the collegewide curriculum committee, which should be attuned to wider standards but may be intolerant of an annoying foreign body complicating its life; and

(d) a special study abroad committee, made up of faculty and staff, which faces the danger of logrolling if made up primarily of "friends."

A frequent compromise involves labeling overseas courses for "general education" or "elective" credit only; or else they are labeled "study abroad" and are viewed as offered by the Study Abroad office, as it were. All courses for "major" credit then require departmental approval. Obviously where the study abroad curriculum is simply the regular campus curriculum delivered without modification overseas, or is the curriculum of another institution accepted intact, this task of curriculum design and approval does not arise.

2. Select and approve instructors

Typically study abroad programs make use of a mix of faculty drawn from the home campus and from elsewhere. In the first instance the hazards are that the least effective faculty members will be off-loaded onto the program, this becoming their salvation in a highly competitive world where they have not flourished in other respects. Second, the most competent faculty are likely to perceive few professional rewards from teaching in study abroad programs and, if they participate at all, they are likely to lose interest quickly. As one program director told us, "You want faculty who are neither too little nor too much interested." Evidently problems of faculty recruitment from the home campus increase with time as the first flush of excitement and romance about service overseas wears off. Moreover, it is especially dangerous for nontenured faculty to take on these assignments, which could cut deeply into the precious time available for research and in most cases reduce substantially the prospects of tenure.

Problems of faculty recruitment off campus are of a different kind. A central role is likely to be played in this process by a program leader or director of study abroad, who will only by accident have professional familiarity with the discipline in question. Departments seem willing often to delegate for study abroad the important function of quality control implicit in the selection of faculty. This may seem an agreeable reduction in complexity in the short run, but it may build up pressure for an explosion of resentment later on.

Interestingly we heard on several occasions from faculty that the main payoff for them in study abroad had been the stimulating teaching environment they encountered overseas. They report an attitude and response among students that they have never experienced before, and strong teacher–student bonds evolve that survive many years. These unexpected benefits should be communicated somehow to desirable candidates for faculty positions.

3. Foster creative imagination

Any vibrant academic unit must constantly be proposing and criticizing new departures in its affairs. The faculty members of a department or school will typically perform this critical role in small groups, or in a committee of the whole. It is important to provide a responsible faculty body (council, committee, etc.) to perform this function for study abroad. Such a faculty body should contain mainly friends of study abroad (enemies will simply be obstructive or destructive), but not exclusively those with a vested self-interest in it. Moreover, provision should be made for regular rotation of membership so that isolation is limited and fresh perspectives are guaranteed. A delicate balance must be discovered between the prerogatives of this faculty body and the authority of those administering study abroad. Care must be taken neither to denature the former nor to paralyze the latter.

4. Identify program directors

Typically each study abroad program operated by a college or university will be directed by a single person, normally but not necessarily a faculty member. Usually this person will reside abroad during the course of the program; in some cases he (or she) may remain on the home campus, and in others may reside abroad permanently. Three problems with directors are reported most often.

(a) They are called upon to perform highly complex tasks for which they are unprepared, and chaos results. They may have to negotiate housing contracts, arrange currency transactions, establish relations with foreign governments, cope with homesickness (or real sickness), and deal with a myriad of crises for which neither their graduate school training nor college experience equipped them.

(b) After an initial flush of enthusiasm they lose interest. Particularly when the pressures of promotion and tenure are upon them, faculty members are unlikely to remain in directorial posts for more than a year or two.

(c) Directors for whom other options have disappeared may be reluctant to give up control of programs. As in the case of the teaching staff special provision should be made to prevent migration of the academically unselected to the administration of study abroad and to assure rotation of responsibilities widely among those with administrative competence.

5. Arrange for academic credit

From the student perspective the most serious challenge in study abroad is to obtain satisfactory credit for academic work completed. For those students enrolled in courses that are simply extensions of the home campus the problem may not exist, although even here some departments may be reluctant to grant credit toward the major. In other cases, where students are enrolled in a relatively autonomous program of the university, take part in the program of another institution or cooperative venture of some kind, or register directly in a foreign institution, the situation is less clear cut. An institution may solve the problem in one of three ways. The problem has two dimensions: commensurability and validation. Parts of the study abroad curriculum simply may not correspond to any offerings on the home campus, so how should they be counted? And, even if the home and foreign offerings are comparable, how and by whom should the overseas performance be evaluated? All this may be left as the student's problem, to solve either before or after the overseas experience. Exact provisions vary, but in most cases this solution is traumatic and threatening to the students. Some faculty with whom we talked thought this was as it should be: character-building and properly discouraging to the faint of heart. (All the evidence we encountered was to the contrary.) Some faculty required prior submission of program descriptions and course syllabi; others asked for presentation of readings, term papers, and examinations completed. Still others required each student to obtain agreement from a faculty member in advance to supervise the entire episode and then certify credit afterward. For students looking forward to graduate or professional school, where a few poor grades let alone a bad semester or year could mean disaster, this kind of unpredictable arrangement can be intolerably risky. When word spreads among the student body that such deleterious effects could materialize, this greatly affects the types and number of students who seek to study abroad.

A second arrangement is for a person on campus – faculty member or administrator – to be delegated authority to approve transfer credit. Such a person, over time, can accumulate great skill and extensive knowledge of the expectations of the local faculty and also of the qualifications of various overseas programs. It is essential, obviously, for a person with this task to build up the trust of faculty. We sensed from our conversations with such persons that they strove usually to be purer than Caesar's wife, and tougher than Caesar himself. It is especially important for professional schools such as business and engineering, because of their accreditation requirements as well as innate faculty skepticism, to assign some person (e.g., an assistant or associate dean) to penetrate and interpret the mysteries of foreign curricula in their fields. One such engineer who spent a substantial part of his time estimating the quality of foreign institutions and the content of their curricula spoke of this as establishing a "matrix of correlation." Typically, he explained, the aggregate curricula of engineering programs covered the same material worldwide; but they did it in different ways, in different sequences, and broken down into different units. His task was to identify comparability. Seldom was it possible, he said, simply to place a junior engineer from his school in the third year of a foreign program. Instead it was necessary usually to pick and choose from the offerings in several years of the foreign curriculum to put together the crucial course material that the student could not afford to miss and still make normal progress toward the degree. However, he emphasized, such a jerry-built arrangement was usually workable and it was well worthwhile.

The third option, in place at some campuses we visited, is to assign responsibility for approval for transfer credit of off-campus programs to a faculty committee. Demanding as this method is for those so designated it does involve faculty effectively in the process and it engenders confidence in cases where faith in the rigorous standards of administration is low.

In general we perceived that transfer of course credit was available to study abroad students on most campuses in the following *descending* order of difficulty:

(a) core technical and scientific courses,
(b) elective technical and scientific courses,
(c) courses for credit toward a major in any field,
(d) elective courses in the humanities and social sciences with little local institutional content (e.g., microeconomics or statistical methods),
(e) electives in the humanities and social sciences with special local relevance (e.g., French economic policy, or modern British authors), and
(f) courses for credit toward graduation. A highly specific ques-

tion, but an important one, is whether study abroad can be counted for residency credit, especially when the program is operated by the home institution.

Tasks for the central administration

6. *Create appropriate administrative structures*

No simple formula or blueprint can be described for an administrative office concerned with study abroad. Indeed, a large general issue is whether it is better to assign administrative tasks of study abroad to the units that perform these functions on campus in general, or whether these tasks should be lodged in a special office for study abroad. In general there are advantages to having study abroad fully embedded and distributed throughout the institution; thereby it gains acceptance, protection, and stability. But disadvantages may be inflexibility, invisibility (in not being a single, detached entity to which people may point), and vulnerability to ill-informed prejudices of faculty and administrators. This question of which place in the structure is best must be kept in mind for each of the administrative functions discussed in this chapter. The optimal structure will depend on the size, mission, character, and history of any given institution. It seems best here merely to discuss some of the issues involved.

For reasons discussed below, it is important to have study abroad well woven into the total fabric of the institution, and the administrator responsible for the function should be firmly in the academic sector, rather than in student affairs, student services, general administration, counseling, or some other more distant part of the educational hierarchy. It is interesting that study abroad programs during their early postwar years tended often to fall under student affairs, reflecting apparently the predominant concern for "proper" student behavior overseas. As the locus of concern changed to the academic integrity of the programs their location in the hierarchy shifted to academic affairs. One program director reported his informal office motto today is "academic respectability and decent concern for student welfare." Whether

the study abroad officer should report to the dean of the undergraduate college (which tends to discourage universitywide participation), to a vice-provost for international programs (if such a
position exists), or to some other comparable figure will depend
on circumstances. For study abroad to prosper, however, it must
not be possible for the officer or the administrator to be easily
ignored. Both problems and possibilities tend to demand urgent
attention when they materialize. In smaller institutions we found
the study abroad office combined often with that of the dean of
students or with the foreign student advisor. Each combination
has advantages and disadvantages. In large and prosperous institutions with a strong commitment to study abroad we sometimes
encountered a director and staff with library, conference and reading rooms, and a handsome suite of offices. These are nontrivial
matters because it is the sad reality, well understood by faculty
and students, that in higher education as in most bureaucracies
the importance attached to a function can be fairly judged by its
physical facilities. One institution we visited had established its
study abroad program as a separate not-for-profit corporation. We
doubt the general applicability of this model.

7. Provide financial aid

Problems both of principle and of practice arise out of the provision
of financial aid for study abroad. An initial question is whether
aid of any kind should be available. For those who see foreign
study as a frivolous act of personal consumption the answer is
"no." But for others the issue is more complex. Should aid, perhaps, be available only for the home university's programs, or
possibly also for other programs that have been "approved" by
the home university? But if study abroad is truly a significant
educational experience, why not aid for all who participate? Yet
if local aid is provided to students who take it elsewhere, what will
be left for the new students who fill their places on the home
campus? Does study abroad mean that the institution's aid budget

must increase, even when the number of tuition-paying students remains constant? As is discussed in Chapter 5, provision of financial aid is closely tied to questions of discrimination in study abroad. If a balance is to be obtained in the students taking part in study abroad, a financial aid policy must be accepted that is at least as generous as that applied to the entire student body.

Problems in the administration of financial aid for study abroad arise because of various restrictions introduced by federal and state governments on uses of funds. In general all federal student aid, with the exception of college work-study, can be applied to study abroad so long as students are enrolled in an "American" program and certain other conditions are met. State restrictions on use of public funds vary from great liberality in some cases to full prohibition in others, especially for registration directly in a foreign institution. For those states with tight restrictions we suggest that the public institutions have a task to convince authorities of the real significance of study abroad. As is often the case with regulation of all kinds those restrictions on use of financial aid have probably warped the pattern of study abroad in ways that were never anticipated by the original regulators. In particular the number of students enrolled in relatively protective American programs giving U.S. credit directly has become greater than it would be otherwise. Conversely the educationally attractive practice of "mainstreaming" has been severely penalized because students are enrolled in foreign institutions through which federal aid may not flow.

One approach to the administration of financial aid for study abroad is to say it will remain with those units of the institution that dispense aid for students as a whole, that is, the financial aid officers at the several colleges and schools. The problem with this approach is that those responsible are likely to be insensitive, and even hostile, to the special needs of overseas students. Another approach is to tell the study abroad programs that they may dispense aid, but must raise from external sources all of their own funds. This approach stirs up the initiative of administrators, some of whom we found had been very successful in raising funds from seemingly unpromising sources such as the business community. However it cuts off study abroad from access to the really big aid sources on campus, which are probably essential to the long-term health of the programs.

Some sort of compromise between these two polar positions – for example, making use of a specialized, sensitive, and sympathetic financial aid officer who has responsibility beyond the study abroad program and has the confidence of higher authorities – seems the wisest course. It is evident that the full support of the central administration and of the governing board is crucial to the development of an effective aid program for study abroad.

A sad fact of academic life, of course, is that financial aid for students may be a much larger problem for public institutions than for private ones. At the privates the tuition and fees of students who study abroad can often cover the full costs of instruction, living expenses, and travel overseas. This source is often not available to the public colleges and universities.

8. Engage institutional leaders

We were struck repeatedly by the importance of a charismatic leader in galvanizing a campus to focus on and undertake study abroad. Usually the key person is the president, but it also may be a provost, dean, state governor, system chancellor, or even some dynamic senior faculty member. Enormous resources are not required to make study abroad work; what are usually lacking where such a program does not exist are vision, a sense of commitment, and a clarion call to action.

Throughout our explorations the effect of a prior foreign experience on the current interest of academic leaders in study abroad kept rising to the surface. From the immediate postwar years these were mainly persons who had been involved in the war and reconstruction. The next generation came out of American efforts to reshape a new world order through the United Nations and its organs, and to assist Third World development through aid agencies of various kinds. The latest generation are veterans of the Peace Corps. Those who have completed a Peace Corps tour seem especially sensitive to the impact of intensive exposure to a foreign culture on the formation of a young American, particularly when combined with some form of social service in the Third World. Peace Corps alumni of the 1960s and 1970s are now sprinkled throughout American higher education and increasingly are arriving at positions of leadership and influence. Whether they are simply those who, with or without the Peace Corps experience, would have been committed to educational exchange cannot be known. But it is undeniable that they approach the subject with special sensitivity and enthusiasm, which makes them a powerful force pressing not only for more foreign experience, but for a new kind of experience – moving beyond the old mold of junior year in Europe to time spent in the Third World.

A major challenge for study abroad at most institutions in the United States today is to become fully embedded in the institutional structure. At the moment it is highly marginal in most institutions, meaning that often it is ill-equipped to get its jobs done and is in danger of retrenchment when times are tough. Only the leadership of an institution can accomplish this embedment by making appropriate administrative appointments and arrangements and by demonstrating its full support. One technique for galvanizing a campus to action is for the president to name a blue-ribbon committee of respected and sympathetic faculty to explore the entire subject of study abroad and make recommendations. Many campuses today have faculty with extensive international experience who are not associated with any of the formal international studies programs. These are a valuable resource for such an inquiry and should not be forgotten. We encountered a half-dozen or so committee endeavors of this kind and found them both enlightened and a sound basis for action in each case.

One veteran of many years of study abroad administration confided that it is not inherently difficult to attract and retain the interest of campus leaders, but it must be done consciously and deliberately. He recommended strongly regular visits by leaders to study abroad program sites, and their involvement in the negotiation of contracts and other instruments. It is not difficult to pick up the infectious excitement of successful study abroad, and there can be few witnesses as effective as a young student whose life has recently been transformed by the experience.

Leadership is appreciated by the troops as well as by the officers of study abroad. On one major campus we visited we heard little more than an unremitting "litany of lamentations and frustrations" about the failure of campus leaders to overcome "parochial attitudes, institutional mismanagement, and local tyranny." Here the troops appealed both for administrative support to their generals and for profound consciousness-raising throughout the army.

9. Facilitate stability with flexibility

Two conditions facing most study abroad programs are, taken together, a recipe for disaster:

(a) The expectation of the authorities is that the programs will at least break even and will not under any circumstances "be a drain" on the rest of the institution,

(b) The world in which these programs operate is characterized above all by uncertainty and unpredictability.

It is worth reflecting a little on each of these conditions and on their implications for study abroad.

Almost all of American higher education is subsidized, either from private gifts and endowments or from the public purse, or from the two together. Therefore, to prescribe that study abroad must "pay for itself" amounts in effect to declaring that it is not really education but is a mere consumption good for which no public subsidy should be allowed. This is a philosophical position consistent with only one of the alternative goals of study abroad, discussed in Chapter 2 (goal 14); it is inconsistent with the others. Simply because study abroad has been recognized for its large potential educational value rather late should not, we suggest, cause it to be excluded from access to central support on the same basis as other educational programs. The arguments used to exclude study abroad from all subsidy include, in private institutions, the revered principle of each new tub on its own bottom, and, in public institutions, the principle that public funds may not be expended outside the state or nation. Neither argument, we suggest, is applicable in this case.

The peculiarly unstable environment in which study abroad programs operate grows out of several conditions. First, American students are notoriously swayed by fashion, and study abroad enrollments may fluctuate accordingly. Italy may be "in" this year and Nepal "out" – just when an institution has invested heavily in a new center in Kathmandu and closed the one in Rome. Second, the world's geography is subject to dramatic vulnerabilities. An institution may organize programs in Mexico and Kiev only to watch helplessly as an earthquake or nuclear accident wipes them out. World politics are equally unreliable. Programs may be set up in Jerusalem or Madrid only to have a Middle East War or threats of indiscriminate terrorism do them in. Finally, the world economy has introduced yet more reasons for heartburn. Carefully calculated revenues and expenses may be knocked into a cocked hat by sudden imposition of exchange controls or rapid shifts in currency exchange rates. The natural volatility of students in reaction to these natural and man-made phenomena is compounded by nervous parents, many of whom believe study abroad is a bad idea in the first place and are glad of an excuse for the coup de grace. The volatility and instability of study abroad is, one suspects, greater in the 1980s, with its many varied and complex programs, than in earlier decades, when language instruction and the grand tour were the principal objectives sought.

There are various ways to limit and constrain the effects on study abroad programs of changing conditions, especially restrictions on freedom of students to withdraw after a certain date. But under even the best of conditions ulcers are likely to be an occupational hazard for those who operate these programs. Of greatest importance is this: If those with ultimate authority do not take steps to cushion change by permitting intertemporal and interprogram financial transfers, and by providing emergency reserve funds, they too will be faced with repeated crises and even ultimate tragedy.

10. Decide whether to go it alone or with others

Many of the schools we visited were attempting to decide at that time whether to increase the amount of their own study abroad programming. The alternative, of course, was to encourage, or at least permit, their students to take part in the programs of others.

The arguments in favor of local programs include the confidence about quality that comes with control, the sense that "surely we can do it better than *that*," the distinction that the institution might achieve thereby, and a chance for various campus entrepreneurs to "do their thing." In addition, of course, for those convinced of the legitimacy of the loftier goals of study abroad discussed above there is as much reason to operate overseas programs oneself as to teach economics or English.

Arguments against running one's own study abroad program are the potentially very large costs, both visible and hidden (the latter mainly in faculty and staff time), and the considerable liability that may be incurred thereby. Not only is a substantial investment constantly in jeopardy in the form of facilities and employment commitments, but the potential legal liability of taking minors into dangerous areas preys on administrators' minds. An obvious but often overlooked factor is that study abroad programs, once set up, do not simply run themselves. They require constant attention for internal and external reasons, and they need regular rejuvenation. Programs seem to experience some economies of scale, and accordingly there is always pressure for growth. One of the regrettable side effects of the perceived benefits from growth is that protectionist sentiments are likely also to grow on the home campus, favoring requirements that the local customers (students) purchase the local product exclusively.

The alternatives to running one's own program are to send students to programs of other colleges and universities and participation in various cooperative endeavors.

In recent years a wide range of collaborative programs of one kind or another has sprung up. These include projects run by large national bodies like the Council on International Educational Exchange, regional cooperatives like the Great Lakes Colleges Association and Associated Colleges of the Midwest, organizations geared to particular kinds of user-institution (e.g., College Consortium for International Studies, a New York City–based organization geared primarily toward the needs of community colleges), and others. If an institution plays a significant role in the collaboration, perhaps placing members on the board or in the administrative structure, it is possible to remain well informed of the conditions there. If not, it is sometimes difficult (and even dangerous) confidently to advise students to enroll. One college told us that, having lost confidence in a cooperative venture, they began systematically to recommend to students that it be avoided. Soon they were informed that the program had sent a "ringer" for advice and, when this was negative, had threatened suit if it were not changed.

The University of California and the State University System in California both conduct their study abroad programs through a "systemwide" office. The extraordinary success of these offices, their demonstrated national leadership, and their widespread popularity among their constituents are most striking. More state systems of colleges and universities should adopt this sensible model for capturing economies of scale. One explanation why it is not more common may lie in the observation made to us several times that systemwide programs must be unusually careful and conservative in style. With so many pairs of eyes upon them they cannot afford to wheel and deal in a way that may be desired by some institutions.

A special problem faced in collaborative programs not within a system but among disparate colleges and universities, especially a mix of public and private ones, relates to tuition. A customary arrangement in such cases is for each student to pay the tuition and fees of the home institution: The costs of the operation are then shared by the participating institutions. When students discover that they are paying widely different amounts for seemingly identical services, bitterness ensues.

We were struck by positions taken by several institutions we visited – positions that, in the aggregate, seem inconsistent and potentially destructive. These institutions all plan to start new overseas programs, or expand existing ones, but are counting upon many students from *other* institutions. They make the persuasive case that their own students benefit almost as much from a rich mixture among their colleagues as from their overseas environment. The potential problem, of course, is that there will not be enough students to go around. Indeed, during the demographic trough of the next few years, if enrollments in study abroad programs do decline on some campuses, we can expect hard-pressed institutions to make it more difficult for their students to join the programs of others.

11. Offer sound advice to students

Study abroad is by its essence an extremely complex subject. Students are exposed to a barrage of propaganda and claims, true and false. One of the basic questions they face is whether it can be done within the constraints of other demands upon their time. The faculty must give a candid and truthful answer early in the students' career and in all their own publications. In addition, vendors, including the home institution, offer to sell students transport, living facilities, instruction, identity cards, insurance, and innumerable other goods and services of uncertain worth. Regardless of how many of these items on the menu an institution is able to provide for its own students, the faculty has a responsibility to them to provide correct information and sound advice about the smorgasbord. Whether the advice comes originally from a faculty member or, more likely, an administrative office, it should be well formulated and readily available.

Advice implies not merely the provision of factual data; it must also convey the atmosphere of study abroad and what may be gained from it. What are the likely effects on personal growth, employment prospects, and admission to graduate school? What are the downside risks as well as the upside gains? How should the student prepare so as to get as much as possible from the experience? What are the current myths on campus and what the reality? At one major state university an explosive growth in overseas programs was attributed to as random a factor as the infectious enthusiasm of one vocal faculty advisor who had herself studied abroad and felt the experience changed her life. This illustrates the potential impact on programs as well as on students of the advisory process.

It is important for every institution to remember always that the study abroad needs of each student may differ from a norm, and few simple formulas can be devised that will apply uniformly. The goals and limitations of each student must be assessed and taken into account. For example, a sophomore with a 2.2 GPA must be fairly warned that a mainstream junior year will almost certainly wipe out chances for admission to law or medical school. The higher administrators must be alert also to and guard against the potential conflict of interest that may cloud the provision of all advice on study abroad. Just as an enrollment-hungry department may counsel against overseas experience for its best undergraduate majors so the desperate director of an undersubsidized study abroad program may counsel universal participation. It is the responsibility of the institutional leadership to operate a system in which the advice offered students reflects their own best interests.

12. Exercise effective oversight

The problem that, more than any other, concerns the academic communities in which study abroad programs are embedded is how to establish effective oversight and continuing quality control. The usual practices of department, school, and faculty appear often to break down in this case. In the view of many faculty, at least, study abroad if neglected falls through the cracks, and is forgotten by those for whom it is a responsibility. In part the problem is simply "out of sight, out of mind": "Who knows what they're up to over there in Siena?" In part it is also the familiar problem of regulation – the regulators soon are "captured" by the regulated. The oversight committee then becomes merely a lobby. In part it is also a reality of American academic life that a universitywide program of this kind does not easily sustain faculty attention. There is no simple answer to this problem. One large research university oscillates between a large oversight committee for all programs (which in due course neglects some of its responsibilities) and smaller committees for each program, which use up inordinate faculty time. Another institution depends heavily on administrative oversight alone. The clear message is, however, that continuing vigilance is the price of quality. One of the costs of not developing an oversight system that is effective over time is to provoke the faculty into periodic bursts of outrage. In our travels we encountered several situations where in recent months faculty inquiries and resulting exposés had imperiled the survival of study abroad on those campuses.

In addition to preserving standards in an absolute sense an effective oversight system will also assist study abroad programs to keep abreast of current practices and changing fashions, and thereby to preserve standards in a relative sense. One of the most serious mistakes any part of an educational institution can commit is to get dangerously out of step with the other parts; this can happen especially easily when the steps are changing rapidly and the one part is geographically several thousand miles from the larger whole.

13. Make it financially feasible overall

Costs of study abroad of all types may vary widely. Variables that explain cost most directly are quality of living accommodation (high for a special facility, low for families and student dormitories), instructional program (high for imported U.S. faculty, low for mainstreamers in most cases), and program direction (high for a U.S. resident director, low for special arrangements with a local person). A general rule we heard expressed in several places is that students will be able and willing to pay the price so long as the total cost of study abroad does not exceed significantly the normal on-campus costs plus excursion airfare. Naturally this rule provides private institutions with much more latitude than public ones. Nevertheless it is striking how successful public institutions have been in developing economically viable programs.

The successful financial operation of study abroad requires adjustment to a range of conditions quite different from those experienced on the home campus, and it is crucial for all parties so to recognize. In addition to the obvious problems of foreign currency variations and foreign tax considerations there are such realities as seasonal variability in enrollment (low in fall, high in spring), sudden changes in student fashion about living in special accommodations, and the need to respond to the financial vagaries of the host educational system as well as to the domestic one. The effective business management of study abroad has become a highly skilled profession not unlike that of the manager of the foreign subsidiary of an American corporation.

14. A mélange of tasks

It is possible to operate study abroad without performing a variety of the administrative tasks discussed here, or without performing them well, but there are likely to be costs of neglect in both the short and long run. Chores that should be undertaken, in addition to those discussed above, include effective publicity, recruitment of students, provision of information to the local community (including videotapes), communication between campus and overseas projects, publication of brochures and newsletters, arrangements for travel and currency exchange, acquisition of real estate, immigration and visa arrangements, maintenance of contacts with alumni, fund-raising, predeparture orientation, continuing negotiation with foreign institutions and governments (no small task, requiring skill and experience), and institutional research for post-audit and program improvement. Institutional research appears especially desirable in this field because of the conviction with which seemingly contradictory positions are held on policy issues. To give only one example, we heard the strongest possible statements about the comparative value of different living arrangements. Some claim that living in homes is the only satisfactory mode; only *there* is a continued use of the language enforced. Others insist that only a local dormitory with a majority of indigenous students provides the peer interaction essential to true mastery of language. Still others say that unless students have available the comfort and reassurance of life in a special dorm with other

Americans the majority will be unable to cope and deal effectively with their instructional program. Surely empirical research will shed light on these several claims.

We suspect that one of the principal hazards in starting and operating a study abroad program comes in underestimating the responsibilities that ensue. The purpose of this chapter has been to give some sense of the range, variety, and challenge of the tasks.

5

Some questions to consider –
great and small

Fundamental questions grow out of the very essence of study abroad and its place in American higher education. No campus leader responsible for these programs whom we met had attempted to answer all these questions, or had even addressed them all systematically. Some have never even heard or imagined the questions. In part this is because of their varied relevance for different campuses, and in part it reflects lack of planning at most institutions. This does not, however, make the questions any less important. It suggests rather that some programs have been less effective than they might have been with straight and clear thinking.

We suggest that any institution with a current or prospective commitment of any magnitude to study abroad should address most of these questions directly and answer them for the particular conditions at that institution. What follows is intended to assist this process. Some of the considerations relevant for each question are sketched out briefly.

Large and unavoidable questions

1. Which approach is right for us?

Every institution should face this question squarely, no matter whether it may seem to have been answered already. Indeed institutions should perhaps reconsider the answer at regular intervals. Conditions and options change so rapidly that there is never a "final solution" for all time. The place to begin to seek an answer to this question is with a candid review of goals. If you do not know where you want to go, you cannot plan how to get there! (Alternatively, if you do not know where you are going, *any* road will take you there!) The process of goal selection must be appropriate for each institution; in most cases, we think it should be conducted as widely, openly, and frankly as possible. Widespread understanding of objectives will at least minimize misunderstandings and disappointments. Some goals, of course, are not those that an institution would like to endorse publicly; but within its own decision-making bodies they should be well understood and accepted. No experienced administrator need be told that a selection among alternative goals cannot be made according to some inevitable logic. The various constituencies of the institution must be considered and their reactions gauged. Faculty may want this, but the students that, while trustees or regents may not accept either without an extended period of persuasion and education.

After one or more goals has been accepted for programs of study abroad, one or more of the alternative styles (or a careful melding of two or more) must be selected for an institutional program. This selection should be consciously taken by the leaders of an institution; there are many individuals, on campus and off, who would like to make the selection themselves with their own self-interest rather than that of the academic community as the main consideration. These persons should be given a part in the process but not the final selection.

A basic issue that must be addressed by each campus answering this question concerns the trade-offs between economies of scale on the one hand and independence and autonomy on the other. Every institution will face a plethora of options for cooperative projects. These, if carefully chosen, may afford wide selections of sites, experienced leadership, sharing of risk, and a relatively slight institutional commitment. On the other hand they will not be "our own" and will almost certainly not be as responsive to special needs as would a unit within the institution, or a wholly owned subsidiary. The potential loss of independence and gain in efficiency holds for participation in a collaboration within a public system as well as for cooperation among wholly autonomous institutions.

A consideration in deciding which approach to take to study

abroad is whence the impetus comes for development and therefore where interest may be expected to continue. We observed cases where pressures came either from students, faculty, or administration – or a combination of two or three. But the initial impetus can change: After development begins to take place, various interactions occur. The students give courage to the faculty; administrators challenge the faculty; and the faculty go their entrepreneurial way.

Another pattern we encountered was where a college lacked the critical mass for its own program, but started one all the same. The pressure here for growth is nearly inexorable and may overwhelm educational arguments that urge otherwise.

2. How élite or discriminatory a focus?
(A privilege or entitlement?)

A charge often made against study abroad programs is that they are among the most discriminatory and élitist features of American higher education. They are designed to serve various select groups rather than to engage the masses. The charge of discrimination is made less on the evidence of overtly restrictive eligibility requirements than on the data of who has actually participated in programs to date. The claims of discrimination are at four levels:

(a) intellectual,
(b) economic,
(c) racial and/or ethnic, and
(d) by age, marital status, and physical handicap.

These charges, and the defenses against them, are examined here one at a time. No attempt is made to reach a conclusion on the merits of the charges; indeed, a final judgment must depend to some extent on personal values and upon the particular circumstances of time and place.

One powerful theme in most discussions of study abroad, as discussed above, is that it should be reserved for those who have prepared thoroughly for it, and therefore presumably can make the best use of it. Students before departing for foreign study, the argument runs, should have a high level of linguistic fluency and cultural sophistication. They should be able and prepared to compete with native students on their own ground and in the institutions where they study. One argument made in defense of this position, in selective colleges at least, is that because we demand a high level of competence from foreign students coming to this country we should expect no less from ours abroad. Another argument is that our students are our cultural ambassadors, and we should send only the very best. If we do not do so, moreover, our students will soon lose their welcome and all will suffer.

The critics of this tough and restrictive position note that the conditions proposed by the "hairshirt mainstreamers" would in fact limit foreign study to those who are intellectually highly gifted. Moreover, these students must be humanistic in orientation or they could not have the time to prepare themselves in the fashion demanded. Why, say the critics, should serious exposure to a foreign educational setting be limited to this intellectual élite? Other educational offerings are increasingly made available to all students without regard to level of accomplishment. Why should there not be a range of packages and various degrees of rigor open for those with varied intellectual capacity? Why should not study abroad be freely available to all who seek it seriously? To the argument that the provision of less rigorous study abroad is to mainstreaming what junk food is to serious nutrition, the critics respond that the sale of several billion Big Macs has not cut into the sale of yogurt and granola.

There seems to be rather wide agreement that study abroad should not be available to the intellectually inferior student. The argument, summarized, is that this student has enough difficulty simply coping with the basics, and a foreign culture could bring catastrophe. Moreover, the effect of this student on the program and on the country in which he/she studies is so negative that rejection can be validated on these grounds alone. At the same time note should be taken of the counterargument on this point, which we heard a number of times. Several program directors report that some students with mediocre records simply come to life after a foreign experience. Whether this transformation results from some personality change or from the effects of new stimulation is unclear. In any event the case for exclusion even of the intellectual nonachiever is not without another side.

It should be recorded also that one program director insists he has just as much trouble with the intellectually very gifted as with the intellectually disadvantaged. The gifted tend to be extremely narrow in their interests, goal-directed, and devoted above all to preserving their grade-point averages. These objectives do not equip them well for the easygoing rough and tumble of much study abroad.

We were reminded during our conversations that this argument about whether to limit a component of higher education to the intellectual élite is as old as the nation. It reflects the contrasting positions of Jefferson and Jackson, the Morrill Act, and the establishment of select private colleges. Just as the argument did not begin with application to study abroad, it will not end there.

The charge of economic discrimination is even more complex than that of intellectual élitism. In simple terms it is pointed out that poor students cannot afford most forms of study abroad. They cannot obtain the extra funds from parents that are often required. Nor can they give up part-time employment or justify to an impoverished family what sounds like a mere junket overseas. Moreover they are essentially "careerists" and can see little relationship between their future careers and foreign experience. At another level some note that the impulse for foreign travel, which resides securely in the American bourgeois life-style, is not present in the low-income family. One urban community college ventured that practically none of their thousands of part-time students had ever traveled abroad or contemplated doing so. A high-quality private liberal arts college, on the other hand, told us that more than 60 percent of their entering freshmen had already been outside the country. Both they and their parents expected to travel much more, and study abroad was simply a natural and obvious way to continue the pattern.

Whereas a reduction in intellectual élitism may be accomplished merely by relaxing the admission requirements and employing educational techniques appropriate for less gifted students, a reduction in economic élitism requires both a commitment of financial aid even greater than that provided on the home campus, and a change in attitude as well. The entire purpose of study abroad may have to be explained sympathetically to the low-income student; and to those with strong career aspirations the relevance to future employment may have to be spelled out.

The charge of discrimination on racial and ethnic grounds is similar to and bound up with the charge of economic élitism. The assertion is that study abroad is fully as useful to ethnic and racial minorities in America as to anyone else. But since the current structure is largely the creation of upper-middle-class white Americans of Western European extraction, it is unattractive to minorities. Neither the style nor the content is likely to appeal to persons of different socioeconomic background and geographic origin. Those with Asian, African, Middle Eastern, and Latin American ancestors, and especially those from working class backgrounds, may not be charmed by a rented college in the Oxford High Street or a villa overlooking Florence. Critics of the current study abroad landscape make the point that marvelous opportunities lie undeveloped in the Third World, offering special characteristics that some minority students might find especially attractive: the opportunity to combine study with service, somewhat on the model of the Peace Corps; open and welcoming cultures with which unsophisticated American students can quickly relate (one old India hand remarked that an American student could learn more in a third-class train journey across India than in any single course on a U.S. campus); and low cost. One college told us that they could mount a semester-long program in Mexico for $400 per student. To those who claim that when Third World study abroad programs are presented few minority students enroll, the response is that this is because these programs are not constructed and marketed with sufficient imagination and sensitivity.

Those who respond to the charges of ethnic and racial discrimination make several points. First, they admit that there is a core of truth to the claims that must be taken into account in future program construction and administration. In particular financial aid must make it as easy as possible for minorities to take part as for others. But the defenders of current programs go on to point out that Third World programs are notoriously difficult to operate successfully. The chaotic conditions in many of the universities in developing countries are a basic problem. If a program is set up on a set of assumptions one day, conditions and the assumptions may change the next. It is often difficult to guarantee the academic integrity of any program over an extended term. Physical hazards are also undeniable. Crime in some Third World cities, especially against foreigners, makes American cities look tame. Political turbulence also may quickly turn into anti-American action, as Iran demonstrated, and an American college or university thousands of miles away is not equipped to take swift protective action. Dietary and health problems, although not necessarily decisive, certainly take on a significance in the Third World that is not matched in Western Europe.

Finally, those who charge discrimination on grounds of marital status, age, and handicap make the point that relatively few study abroad programs have been constructed so that it is practical for persons with families (especially single parents), older persons, the handicapped, or even married persons to take part. Timing, living arrangements, miscellaneous requirements, all seem geared to the young, unattached, highly mobile students with few commitments, responsibilities to others, or other inhibitions. We did detect some concern for this problem in our conversations. The community colleges in particular were designing programs aimed at these potentially neglected groups.

One institution emphasizes that it exercises "selection" rather than discrimination. They admit to study abroad on the basis of personality, motivation, background, adaptability, and likely response to crisis. The point remains, nevertheless, that even in this case study abroad is deemed to be appropriate only for some subset of those students admitted to that institution. This most benign form of discrimination is a widely held position.

One of the insidious features of discrimination in study abroad, as in other parts of society, is that it feeds on itself. So long as programs are perceived to be designed and reserved for the unusually talented, wealthy, young, and white, these are the participants who will tend to apply. Moreover, because those with some international experience already are most likely to undertake study abroad, lack of this experience, like the cycle of poverty, becomes self-reinforcing. Extra efforts must be made, then, to restore the mix of the program. All this being said we did see considerable evidence that imaginative nondiscriminatory new programs are being undertaken, especially in Third World countries, and the prospect for their growth is excellent. Other causes of discrimination are also being recognized and combated.

3. Can integration within the institution be accomplished?

The international dimensions of a contemporary American college or university include some or all of the following: foreign students on the campus; foreign language and area studies; international elements in many curricular offerings and research projects, especially in such fields as international relations; faculty visits overseas; international assistance contracts; and study abroad. To a striking degree these activities are all conducted independent of each other. We are fully aware of the long tradition of decentralization in American higher education and of the inherent conservatism that protects the system from the waves of fashion that affect intellectuals. All the same we find this condition of decentralized autonomy perhaps the greatest threat to study abroad by perpetuating its marginality and by limiting its overall effectiveness.

It is clear that in principle there are innumerable ways in which study abroad may be enriched, and may itself contribute more to the entire educational process, through closer relationships with the other international activities on campus. Ideally the process of an integrated "international education" might be thought of as having three parts. First, students early in the educational process would be exposed to different aspects of the foreign arena to which they will later go, including the language and culture. They will, furthermore, study large issues of world affairs and the analytical skills needed to understand them. They will also become a junior member of the internationalist community on campus, learning of the research interests of faculty and more advanced students and meeting visitors. Second, at some time prior to departure overseas students should be provided a specific orientation that will prepare them for what they will find and how to make the best of it. At Boston University we heard this orientation compared to preparation for an Outward Bound experience in which the emphasis is on self-reliance and agility above all.

With this in the background the period of time a student spends abroad would become a natural extension of earlier studies and experiences. The third part of an international education, the so-called reentry to the home culture, may be at the same time the most difficult and the most rewarding. If time abroad is during the junior year as an undergraduate, there is one year remaining before graduation in which to gain perspective on that experience. This may be accomplished through special reentry seminars, but also through a more sophisticated reimmersion in the internationalist community of interested faculty and other students, including foreign students. A student recently returned from abroad should have both heightened interest and increased sensitivity to issues of concern to this internationalist community. Such a student might usefully be housed on his own campus with foreign students from the region he has recently visited. If a constructive involvement is arranged – including perhaps participation in faculty research and orientation of both future students abroad and new foreign students – then a student's earlier overseas experience is given greater meaning and value. Indeed, we were told that some years ago at the University of Chicago a regular seminar was established that discussed in an analytical fashion the experiences of returned students and the means by which their perspectives were broadened. The returned student who is simply ignored is likely to feel angry, discouraged, and rejected – almost like the returned veteran, on a milder scale.

It should, perhaps, be recognized openly and candidly that although great potential synergism exists among the different parts of many campuses concerned with area studies, foreign students, and study abroad, long-standing (but by no means universal) indifference toward each other, sometimes approaching enmity, exists among the three. In general, area studies is oriented toward serious graduate education and research; foreign students from the area under study are likely to be interested in other things on the American campus; and study abroad participants are often at too low a level of sophistication to be interesting to area specialists. The foreign student advisor has little occasion for contact with area studies, and spends full time protecting and defending the interests of his/her hard-pressed charges; some even believe that most study abroad is merely a diversion of the idle rich. The study abroad officer is usually the most likely member of the triumvirate to stretch out hands to the other two; but once ignored or rebuffed is unlikely to try again.

Some of the campuses we visited had done far more than others in arranging for the constructive integration of study abroad with other international activities and thereby into the mainstream of higher education. However we did not see any single paragon institution and there remains still an ideal yet to be achieved. Until much progress is made in this direction, it appears that study abroad will stay intellectually as well as administratively marginal on the American campus, and the experience not fully part of a student's education.

4. Is extension possible throughout the disciplines and professions?

The case for study abroad in the humanities and social sciences needs hardly to be made: The languages, cultures, and social processes of the rest of the world are the grist for their mills. But how about physics, chemistry, biology, engineering, the health sciences, agriculture, and the innumerable other fields that populate an American campus? Here the case must be made most carefully and reviewed skeptically. One prominent scientist asked us rather pointedly, "How will study abroad help me or my students win a Nobel Prize or get in the National Academy?" On the other hand it was suggested to us by another scientist that mainstreaming abroad was, at least, an ideal experience for premedical students. Nothing duplicated more closely the experience of a patient in a modern hospital than that of the American student dropped into a foreign university, lacking self-confidence, understanding only scraps of the language, and having to cope with colleagues who seemed simply too busy for anyone else's problems. From this experience, it was argued, medical students would learn empathy and humility, serving them in better stead than an extra course in biochemistry.

We heard an interesting discussion at a major technical university at which the scientists and engineers said they visited Japan almost as often as other parts of this country. What more could they gain, they asked, through a sophisticated understanding of the language and culture? To this the Japanologist replied "a great deal." "American technical people abroad," he said, "see the technology embedded in a black box. In attempting to understand what they see they are operating with one tied arm, one patched eye, and a clogged ear." This area studies specialist had established an intensive program that turns out to be exceptionally popular with science-based students, suggesting that scientific disinterest in larger dimensions of study abroad may be generational. A new generation of young scientists may be prepared to stretch out beyond their disciplines. In the culture of the sciences, especially at the graduate level, where all instruction has a precise purpose and is usually supported by an external funding agent, study abroad is now an alien practice. Not only is the benefit from study abroad not obvious, but students are usually encumbered prior to the general examinations with "lockstep" curricula that make such innovations extremely difficult. After these examinations, they are often attached to a mentor who is unlikely to sense the value of overseas experience and whose external funding does not permit students to stray far from the home laboratory. In a way the tasks ahead for study abroad with respect to the sciences are like those of a process in evolutionary biology. A variety of programs, as of species, should compete in a natural selection, with the fittest – meaning the most rigorous and relevant – surviving. Both institutional and national policy in the years ahead should attend to both these elements of the process. Resources should be found to support innovative experiments, and then these experiments should be tested by the most rigorous criteria. Those programs found wanting should be eliminated. This point is made forcefully here because we perceive that the institutional pressures may be all in the other direction: Imaginative experimentation is the exception rather than the rule.

Among the professions law is an interesting special case. On the surface one might expect legal training to be an obvious place for study abroad, for at least three reasons. First, the law itself is based on universal principles with common roots outside the United States. Therefore, an examination of the origins of the law where it began, and of the variants that have evolved in different cultures, should provide a deeper understanding of our own system. Second, the world economy and society, with which lawyers are increasingly concerned, are becoming more and more central to American life. Even a small town lawyer in rural North Carolina is likely today to have a German or Japanese client, or an American client with German or Japanese problems. It would help in such circumstances, one might think, to know something about the German and Japanese societies and their legal systems. Third, the bar has traditionally provided a high proportion of the leaders of society, and especially our legislators. Increasingly the issues with which these leaders deal are international in scope. Therefore, one might expect this internationalization to permeate legal training. But it does so to a very limited degree. Neither international nor comparative law, let alone the wider global context in which the law is embedded, has a significant part in most American legal education. Furthermore, and of greatest relevance to this inquiry, there is relatively little provision for study abroad by law students. In 1986, thirty-nine approved foreign *summer* programs were conducted by American law schools but only four *semester* abroad programs (*Syllabus*, XVII, No. 4, December 1986, p. 2). Law professors themselves travel widely and exchange posts, but they make it difficult for their students to do so at least during the regular term. The reasons they give are that

(a) the domestic curriculum is too demanding to permit a semester or more away;

(b) foreign libraries are inadequate;

(c) even in the summers, jobs with prospective employers are too important (both for the income and the later employment offers they bring) to be sacrificed for a foreign experience;

(d) knowledge of foreign law in the final analysis is not all that useful;

(e) law schools try to pick students who have already gained some foreign exposure; and

(f) they are constrained by accreditation rules from very much overseas experimentation.

Regardless of the strength of these arguments we cannot help observing that paradoxically, in view of the history of the profession, the law school today is the most conservative part of the American campus with respect to study abroad.

It is worth remarking that whereas one relatively low-status profession – secondary-school teaching – is today mandating cross-cultural studies, a high-status profession – the law – makes such studies nearly impossible.

Lesser but important questions

5. What about reciprocity?

Study abroad until recently has been seen as mainly a one-way street. Foreign students aplenty have come to American colleges and universities, but in most cases they come from countries in the Third World, other than those to which American students wish to go. So long as the numbers of Americans abroad remained small there seemed little reason to worry about a two-way flow. Recently, however, as the numbers have increased and the phenomenon of study abroad has come to be taken more seriously, a case can be put forward on behalf of mandating reciprocal flows. Indeed some institutions have come to insist (within limits) upon it. The arguments are based in part on principle and in part on practical considerations. As a general rule, it is claimed, a one-way flow is exploitive. Study abroad then becomes the "mining" of one culture by another, a cruel manifestation of cultural imperialism. Students abroad are then only a sophisticated type of tourist, gawking not just at the natives and their funny ways but in greater depth at their language, society, and culture as well. At a more practical level those who have administered study abroad find that reciprocity can improve the entire tone and effectiveness of the experience. Under a two-way relationship American students become partners and collaborators rather than charges. Moreover, if reciprocity involves the two-way flow of faculty and administrators as well as of students, the host institution abroad will probably accumulate over time an entire community of interested and sympathetic persons who will stand receptive to and understanding of the American students' special problems and needs. Visitors from the foreign institution on the American campus will also constitute a valuable resource for those students yet to depart as well as for those who have returned.

At the same time it has become clear in recent years that traditional forms of one-for-one reciprocity do not often work very well. Costs, institutional regulations, academic quality, and student needs vary so widely among institutions that a simple "exchange" will likely become a Procrustean bed with few people sleeping in it. Typically the bulk of American demands are for undergraduate experiences overseas, whereas most foreign institutions wish to send either advanced graduate students for specialized studies or young faculty for refreshment or completion of a graduate degree. An increasingly popular device we encountered in several institutions was to accumulate dollar credits at agreed exchange rates for services rendered by foreign institutions to American undergraduate students. These credits would then be used by the foreign institutions in a variety of mutually agreeable ways, including participation by their students in degree programs and visits by their faculty as postdoctoral fellows. Such flexible "banking" arrangements appear to be far more attractive to colleges and universities in the United States and abroad than are provisions for direct reciprocal tuition waivers.

Some of the foreign institutional hosts of American students, or at least those entrepreneurial hustlers on the foreign campuses who make the arrangements, have little interest in sending their own students abroad, or at least to the United States. Their interest in negotiating the inward flow is to use facilities profitably during slack periods and to achieve financial benefits. These persons are quite happy to stop there, and reciprocity with them is impossible.

We conclude that in most cases it is not practical to follow the principle of reciprocity slavishly; but as a strong imperative, to be observed wherever possible, it is exceptionally important. Some of the most effective mechanisms for study abroad we encountered were long-established linkages that had grown and flourished with enthusiasm and tender care on both sides. In several cases (e.g., the Universities of Illinois and Massachusetts) major research universities in this country are sending their undergraduates to a developing Third World institution, and at the same time training and retraining the young faculty of this institution. We could see emerging here relationships with a depth and strength comparable to those that have grown up since World War II under AID contracts. We feel confident that in the years ahead such relationships must be the wave of the future.

6. Is geographical balance possible?

Closely related to issues of élitism, discrimination, and reciprocity is the question of how to develop overseas programs in countries that currently are out of fashion with American academe or that may not appeal to students for reasons that are educationally unsound. We were reminded that in recent years media coverage of much of the globe, and especially of the Third World, is largely negative. Readers, listeners, and viewers are reminded incessantly of riots and revolutions, drug cultivation, famine, disease, and anti-Americanism. One result is a prevailing distaste and fear among students and their parents for residence in these countries. There are excellent educational reasons why study abroad should be conducted in Paris, Florence, and Oxford; but a strong case can be made also for Buenos Aires, Istanbul, and Singapore. Moreover, the irony was pointed out to us several times that although the vast majority of American study abroad is in Europe this is the part of the globe where cultural difference is least and should be grasped most easily without on-site residence.

It will undoubtedly take a strong interventionist hand to shift the balance away from Western Europe. At one college we visited special financial aid was afforded students venturing to the Third World. We suspect more actions of this kind would be required to change the distribution markedly. Mexico is the most obvious case in point. This neighbor offers a rich cultural heritage, an excellent training ground for Spanish, remarkably low costs, and the opportunity to cement international relations of enormous significance to the United States. Yet few programs have been established there by American colleges and universities or are in prospect for reasons that we do not fully understand. The two geographic thrusts of the Reagan administration toward the Caribbean Basin and Pacific Rim have both appealed to study abroad enthusiasts as ways of breaking the "Western European dominance" in study abroad. Other devices should be explored. Merely an improvement in information about opportunities outside Europe might help.

This question, we think, deserves much more discussion and attention than it has received to date.

7. Is cross-subsidization justified?

Just as on any campus the costs of different kinds of education vary and are often not reflected in the tuition and fee structure, so the expenses of various projects of study abroad differ and in their pricing raise the same questions of distributional justice. Typically it costs many times more to send a student to Japan and sustain him/her there than to, say, Mexico. Usually the costs to students of these programs reflect these differentials, but seldom fully. On some campuses we visited there was considerable bitterness about comparative rates. Those associated with less expensive programs complained that they were subsidizing the costly ones, and they asked why. We think it wise for the authorities to have an answer ready.

8. How to penetrate public consciousness?

The marginality of study abroad is a problem not only in the educational system and the institutional structure but in the larger public conception of higher education as well. So long as this is the case study abroad is in peril. The task for the leaders of higher education is to wage an educational campaign that will not be completed overnight but should proceed over several years. In the public sector this will require persuasion of regents and legislators that it is advantageous to the state to offer its young this contact with the world. In the private sector the permanence of study abroad requires in particular the acquisition of endowment funds in support of study abroad, both to cover the continuing needs for these programs and to certify their status equal to that of the other endowed programs on campus. Ironically, during the early years of private higher education the endowment of special "traveling scholarships" was a popular form of memorial by donors. It would be appropriate to restore this practice.

We were impressed to hear testimony from a few fund-raisers about how potentially easy study abroad was "to sell." They told, in particular, about the effectiveness of returned students in demonstrating the program's value. The life change that is often reported by these students in the literature evidently comes through to money-givers and the excitement and enthusiasm of the recent returnee becomes profoundly infectious.

9. Should a foreign student study abroad?

One of the consequences of having more than 300,000 foreign students in the United States is that many of them apply themselves for inclusion in study abroad programs at their American host institutions. We encountered widely differing institutional positions on these requests. Some said "no," on the ground that one adjustment to a foreign culture is enough for any student during a course of study. Moreover, when government-sponsored exchanges are involved in an American study abroad program the host government will often object at not receiving "real Americans." One purpose of these exchanges is usually to reflect U.S. foreign policy, and for this another foreign student will not do. We did not discover any distinct position on this question by the sponsors of foreign students in this country, if indeed they have one.

But at the same time we heard numerous accounts of how foreign student participation in study abroad had gone very well, enriching both the foreign students and the programs. In one case a Mexican student enlivened an "enclave" in Spain, providing a link with the Spaniards. In another case a South Korean student was admitted to a program in China, providing a rare point of contact between these two countries. In still another case a Canadian was exposed effectively to South Africa from an American perspective.

10. How long is long enough?

Study abroad varies in length from a few weeks to several years. The optimum length of time clearly varies with circumstances and objectives. A few rules of thumb have been suggested. In general either mainstreaming, or serious study of any kind in the Third World, requires a year or more. At the other extreme experiential learning of various types in the developed world can be accomplished effectively in a semester or quarter. Intensive language programs and projects related to particular courses or fields can be completed in as little as six weeks. Each case requires its own careful scrutiny.

11. Should alumni study abroad?

Those who think that study abroad, like youth, is wasted on the young, have done some thinking about programs for adult alumni. These proposals amount, in essence, to extensions of the alumni travel that is now so widely successful. The experience is simply made sufficiently serious to qualify for postgraduate credit. If the time required is lengthy, of course, the clientele must be mainly retired persons. But we heard of vestigial proposals also for structured "sabbatical years" overseas for successful doctors, lawyers, and other professionals. This approach to the subject requires very careful planning, but it may respond to a growing need and open up major new opportunities for the field.

12. Can we overcome the constraint of postgraduate debt?

Many thoughtful observers conclude that for most students the best moment for study abroad comes not during the junior year but just after the bachelor's degree. At that point the graduates' characters are formed, they are secure in their own culture, and they have some of the tools with which to make sense of a foreign experience. Ideally, these observers suggest, the students should study abroad when they are no longer encumbered by enrollment in an American degree program. In the best of all worlds most students would spend their year overseas after the A.B. but before proceeding to graduate or professional school. One of the main obstacles to this practice today, apart from the absence of institutional mechanisms to facilitate it, is the burden of debt many students accumulate during their undergraduate years. This debt not only prevents them from "taking a year off," during which time interest must be paid, but it impels them to complete their postgraduate studies just as quickly as possible with no unnecessary detour (such as study abroad) along the way. They and their parents cannot afford to incur even more debt. This unintended effect of the debt financing of higher education should be kept in mind when policy toward it is formed.

13. When is the right time?

The junior year abroad came into vogue at the dawn of education overseas, and like so many original cultural forms it has gained a hallowed and "traditional" status in American academe. But is it necessarily the right stage in educational development for foreign experience? Undoubtedly for many it is; but we are persuaded that for many it is not. At the institutional level we have reported on imaginative programs that have come both earlier and later in the academic life course than the junior year. Institutions that are constructing study abroad programs for the first time should not be constrained by a junior-year fetish but should explore the pros and cons of different periods for their own circumstances. All kinds of new departures may be possible in time including, for example, an extended and interrupted educational experience abroad consisting of several pieces and including part-time enrollment and employment abroad.

6

Innovation: the origin of constructive change

Some of the most precious characteristics of American higher education today are its diversity, its resilience, and its capacity to adapt to altered circumstances. These features are sustained by the creative energies of academic innovators and entrepreneurs who respond to changing conditions with new institutional forms. A danger that faces study abroad, as it does other parts of higher education, is that orthodoxy instead of continued innovation will prevail, that a conservative mentality will take hold, dictating that "this, and this alone, is the way to do it." This conservatism is one of the great threats and potential costs of the study abroad bureaucratic establishment that is beginning to emerge in American higher education today. Such an establishment, of course, helps to enforce standards and protects from charlatans and harebrained ideas; but it may also simply repudiate and reject all that is "not invented here." Every effort must be made – including those of academic administrators not directly concerned with study abroad programs – to ensure that tradition does not stand in the way of new ideas and new approaches from outsiders in this young field, an enterprise that has so much to gain from dynamism and flexibility.

In our travels we ran across numerous applications of study abroad that were unusual and imaginative in a large variety of ways. We think it likely that some of these will catch on and be replicated or adopted in part elsewhere. Others will never seem attractive beyond the original institution's walls, and still others will die where they rose, leaving hardly a trace. That is as it should be. The importance here is in the fact of vigorous innovation more than in the inherent merit of particular programs themselves.

To illustrate the range and variety that remain a feature of the national scene, we describe in this chapter nine innovative applications of the study abroad concept that we encountered in our travels. We do not put these forward as some sort of All-American list, but rather as an illustrative menu of food for thought.

In the liberal arts

1. Discover your cultural heritage: the Rome Program of the University of Dallas

The University of Dallas, a small Catholic university founded in its present form only in 1956, is "dedicated to the renewal of the Western heritage of liberal education and to the recovery of the Christian intellectual tradition." In 1970 the University instituted a one-semester program in Rome for sophomores as an integral part of the undergraduate tradition. Courses in the undergraduate core curriculum are taught in Rome primarily by University of Dallas professors making use of the rich artistic and cultural environment around them. The *Bulletin* explanation for the program is as follows.

> We are all of us still, in a sense, as T. S. Eliot has said, citizens of the Roman empire, for Rome brought together the Judaeo-Christian revelation and the classical wisdom to form that Europe which was the progenitor of American ideals. Thus, to a student in the Western World – to seek one's true heritage in the liberal arts – is to follow the path to Rome.

The Dallas program is constructed, unlike most study abroad programs, as a foundation for later education rather than as an extension. All sophomores with a 2.0 GPA are encouraged to take part regardless of major, and about 80 percent do. The program philosophy is thus one of entitlement, not privilege. Financial aid is available and every effort is made to see that all students who would like to go can do so. A tour of Greece is provided, in addition, and the broad Greco-Roman heritage is stressed throughout the curriculum. A hotel complex on the edge of Rome provides living accommodations, classrooms, offices, and library. Typically between 180 and 220 students take part each year, spread between the two semesters. The extra cost of the semester for each student is air travel to Rome.

The Dallas faculty have a distinctive conception of the liberal arts emphasizing the Greco-Roman contribution, and especially the texts of Aristotle, Augustine, and Aquinas. They find that the appreciation they can engender for these texts, when presented on-site as it were, is vastly enhanced over what it would be in Dallas. Moreover, subsequent instruction in art and architecture, philosophy, theology, European history, and modern Italian language and culture are fundamentally improved.

On most campuses study abroad is still reserved for a special few and perceived as a supplement to the regular curriculum. The Rome Program of the University of Dallas demonstrates how study abroad can be made an integrated central feature of college life.

2. Go for broke on a global stage: Regent's College in London of Rockford College, Illinois

The most startling and institutionally ambitious use for study abroad that we encountered on our travels was at Rockford College in Rockford, Illinois. This small but venerable liberal arts college (the alma mater of Jane Addams) has had problems in recent years. Most important, its enrollment of full-time students fell from over a thousand to about seven hundred and fifty in 1986. An energetic new president, Norman Stewart (since departed), pressed a variety of innovations to cope with this crisis – some ill-fated, like an engineering school and "Weekend College," others more successful, such as an MBA degree. But by far the most dramatic gamble by Rockford is acquisition of "Regent's College" in London, the former campus of Bedford College, a constituent unit of the University of London in Regent's Park. Images are conjured up easily from the corporate world to illuminate this development. In one sense Rockford is becoming a truly multinational institution, like IBM or General Motors. In another its acquisition of Bedford (Regent's) is rather like little Capital Cities Broadcasting's recent takeover of the American Broadcasting Corporation.

Rockford has assigned a central role to Regent's College in its future. It hopes for several positive outcomes.

(a) An exceptionally attractive study abroad opportunity may attract excellent and more diverse students to the Rockford campus.

(b) Good students may be wooed away from other American institutions both to study at Regent's and then to return to the Rockford campus. The goal is for a program of one hundred students in three years, one half from other colleges.

(c) The formidable task of organizing and operating Regent's can energize, internationalize, and stimulate the home campus and its faculties. Much of the teaching at Regent's will be by British academics, but Rockford faculty will have overall responsibility.

(d) Foreign students can be attracted first to study at Regent's and then to come to Rockford.

(e) With ample space and attractive facilities a number of promising options may be pursued, for example a program of American-style higher education in Britain leading either to enrollment in a U.S. college or to a Rockford (Regent's) degree (e.g., the MBA). In the meantime the new Regent's College is leasing facilities to a range of other study abroad programs and to various British educational activities.

(f) In a sense, after an extended period of becoming increasingly parochial and insular, the Regent's College move may assist Rockford to return quickly to its long-standing internationalist tradition, based first in missionary activities of the Congregational Church and including participation in the foundation of Kobe College in Japan.

The long-term Rockford commitment in London is limited to a renewable five-year lease of the facilities, which are owned by the Crown. Profit is clearly not a Rockford goal; we were told they would be "tickled to death to break even." One of the evident benefits of the experiment thus far has been to attract and retain several faculty and administrators with an exceptionally strong commitment to education overseas. Two of the new leaders are graduates of Kalamazoo College, where study abroad has a major place in college life. The development staff of Rockford are hopeful of attracting funds that otherwise would not come to the college. They have started an eight-million-dollar fund drive, with half to come from the United States and half from the United Kingdom. The anthropologist Richard Leakey is an active Rockford trustee and Chairman of the Regent's Council; he is felt to symbolize the evolving international orientation of the college.

Clearly there is not unanimous enthusiasm on the Rockford campus for the Regent's College idea. Some regret the distraction of administrators and faculty from domestic problems, and some fear the size of the gamble. But others feel that Rockford has "found its renewal" through this device. Initially, at least, a solid majority of trustees, administrators, students, and faculty were behind the experiment. At most colleges and universities in the United States what distinguishes study abroad clearly is its marginality. At Rockford and at a handful of other institutions with comparable commitments it is possible to see what happens when this condition is reversed.

In science and technology

3. See chemistry from a multinational perspective: the interchange program of the University of Massachusetts and University of East Anglia

Typically most natural or physical scientists with whom we met could see little in study abroad that would benefit their students, especially undergraduates, as scientists. Students might be enriched as human beings, we were told, and they might reasonably take social science or humanities electives abroad, but there was nothing they could gain from doing or learning science anywhere else but on the home campus. We found a marked exception to this position at the University of Massachusetts at Amherst, which has established a successful exchange program with the University of East Anglia at Norwich in chemistry.

First of all it must be noted that the background conditions are exceptionally strong for a relationship between these two institutions. Both have an extended tradition of educational exchange and the University of Massachusetts has the infrastructure and the direction to experiment with promising ideas of this kind.

The secret to the success of this program appears to be just the right mix of similarity and difference between the two partners. Both institutions are relatively rural, of medium size, and open to innovation. Chemical Sciences at East Anglia offers a three-year professional degree. The University of Massachusetts offers the traditional four-year liberal arts degree with a chemistry major. Beginning in 1979 the two departments arranged for exchanges for periods of a year for a few of their best students. In any year between two and twenty move back and forth. The University of Massachusetts at Amherst exchangees pay fees for tuition, room, and board that are comparable to University of Massachusetts at Amherst fees. They also pay travel. Grades received in Britain by the University of Massachusetts students appear "in translation" on their transcripts but do not count in their GPA.

Evidently there are three major benefits from the exchange. First, the students themselves are faced with, and forced to come to grips with, different ways of learning and of conducting science. The East Anglia system involves intensive modular teaching of material, a problem-solving posture, and considerable personal contact between faculty and student, in contrast to the traditional American system of rather formal lectures and laboratory sections. Students on both ends of the exchange find this contrast challenging and stimulating. Careful selection of high-quality exchange participants ensures that they can handle the difference. Second, the two departments, because of the need to mesh their programs for purposes of the exchange, were compelled to make "forced" program reviews, which they might not have done otherwise. Moreover, during the review they had an alternative model facing them at the other institution, against which they were encouraged to judge their own practices.

Third, over time, through the necessity to build trust and a basis for cooperation, other departmental relationships have evolved, including joint research.

Clearly this innovative program requires hard work, commitment, and flexibility to succeed; but it suggests that other demanding experiments in science are possible.

4. Place technology in a comparative context: International Minor in Engineering at the University of Illinois

Most faculty and administrators of professional technical and technological schools with whom we spoke argued that the tasks of coping with peculiar foreign cultures were not proper problems for their students. Perhaps the responsibility for such matters lay with business managers, lawyers, or area studies specialists. The engineer's function, they said, was to design and to build things, not to worry about the larger culture in which this construction was embedded. Of particular significance to us, of course, was the implication of this argument that there is no purpose in a technical professional either studying about or in a foreign land.

A pronounced exception to this position was visible at the College of Engineering at the University of Illinois, one of the most highly respected and selective engineering schools in the world. The college disputes directly the premise accepted elsewhere. It tells entering freshmen that they "will probably spend a portion of their professional career on foreign assignment" and "will have to be able to deal with the increasingly stiff competition of firms outside the U.S." To prepare students to meet these challenges when they graduate, the College of Engineering is now offering an International Minor, in which students combine courses in a foreign language, the culture, economics, and politics in another part of the world with regular engineering studies. Students who have obtained language proficiency in high school – which, interestingly, most Illinois engineers have done – find no difficulty completing the full program in the regular four years of undergraduate study. Each student in the minor must select one non–English-speaking part of the world for concentrated attention; these are listed as Africa, China, Germany, Japan, the Middle East, the Slavic world, South Asia, and Latin America and the Caribbean. Requirements of the international minor include some level of language fluency, a minimum of twenty-one hours of area studies, of which at least nine must be other than language credit, and one course or more in comparative economics or political science. Of special interest for us is the requirement that at least eight weeks must be spent in residence in the chosen geographical area of concentration "to work, study, or serve an internship." The College has a small fund that is used to pay the international travel of students who require assistance (up to fifty awards a year). The college participates in the International Association for the Exchange of Students for Technical Experience (IAESTE) to help in arranging internships.

The moving force in this program to date is Associate Dean Howard Wakeland, an agricultural-civil engineer with extensive service on technical assistance projects abroad. The College, like most others of its kind, has participated in several exchange programs, going back to the 1950s. The International Minor, he says, results from more recent recognition that with their exceptionally talented student body they have a responsibility to offer "engineering education" rather than simply "engineering technology." The International Minor grew out of the College's expectations of what challenges leaders in the engineering world will face over the coming decades. The program began only recently and has sixty students enrolled already. Wakeland emphasizes that they do not propose or claim to turn out from this relatively brief exposure a "finished" area specialist; but the graduates do have more than a rudimentary acquaintance with one region of the world, and a basis for later learning. Already employers are showing a strong positive attraction to those graduates who have completed the International Minor.

Wakeland is a most committed and persuasive advocate of international experience for engineers, and he suggests use of the revenues from the enrollment of foreign engineering students (at potential market prices, not public university tuition rates) to pay for the overseas ventures of American students. A key to the success of the program is the apparent willingness of the administration to permit Dean Wakeland free rein in developing and implementing the program.

The evident success of this imaginative program in engineering at the University of Illinois, one of the most demanding technical programs in the country, demonstrates the potential popularity of international studies and study abroad even in the most unpromising of circumstances.

5. *Look to the east for wisdom:*
MIT–Japan Science and Technology Program,
Massachusetts Institute of Technology

While the International Minor in Engineering at the University of Illinois reflects visionary engineers reaching out to the social sciences and humanities to enrich their education, at the Massachusetts Institute of Technology an MIT–Japan Science Program directed by a political scientist, Richard J. Samuels, has reached out to students in science and engineering to afford them a significant overseas experience. The ultimate carrot for the students to participate in the program is a one-year internship (sometimes extended) in a Japanese firm or laboratory. Prior to that these students must take the equivalent of at least two years of Japanese language study (in special courses using scientific and technical themes) and are encouraged to participate in an interdisciplinary curriculum in Japanese science, society, economics, politics, and history. Each year up to twenty internships are available in such places as Hitachi, Toshiba, NEC, Matsushita, Tokyo University, and various National Laboratories. Samuels reports strong demand from both students and host institutions for the internships. One of the goals of the program is to coordinate and encourage collaborative research associations between the United States and Japan, and it is hoped the internships may lead to more in this direction. Major support for this program has come from about a dozen large American corporations. Evidently both United States sponsors and Japanese hosts see this program as a device for building bridges for the future. Like so many current educational leaders who are enthusiastic supporters of study abroad, Samuels was himself a participant in an undergraduate exchange at Colgate University that he thinks changed his life.

In the article "Applied Japanese Studies for Science and Engineering at American Universities," Samuel K. Coleman of North Carolina State University and Samuels point out the opportunities for a wide range of American technical fields to take advantage of an increasing volume of high-quality research in Japan (*Engineering Education*, January 1986). But most specialists are unable to acquire scientific and technical information because of poor language skills and little comprehension of "the broader context in which Japanese research and development takes place." Coleman and Samuels surveyed the fifteen National Resource Centers for East Asian International Studies (Title VI, Higher Education Act) and found that only at three (Illinois, Ohio State, and Princeton) did science and technology majors make up more than 20 percent of the students enrolled in Japanese language courses. Their sampling led them to "guess there are no more than 400 scientific and technical specialists-in-training now receiving Japanese language instruction in the United States." Moreover, even this small enrollment

> ... is almost entirely the result of student initiative. This initiative is particularly striking given competing curricular demands and the absence of explicit recruitment efforts. There is virtually no internship and fellowship support for science and engineering majors at the leading centers of Japanese studies. There are likewise no courses in technical Japanese. We infer that the dearth of science and engineering students who have a dual concentration in Japanese studies is at least partly attributable to this lack of active marketing.

What is said here about Japanese Studies could undoubtedly be said with equal or stronger emphasis about other linguistic areas. The success of the MIT program suggests that large opportunities lie open for outreach by the nation's area studies programs into centers of strength in science and technology, with study abroad in the various regions as a central feature.

Graduate and professional

6. Find the world is your oyster:
Joint Program leading to the M.B.A. degree and the M.A. degree
in International Relations at the University of Chicago

One of the problems with providing for an overseas experience in a professional degree program is that it may be too superficial to be useful. Not only is the time short for any nontraditional activities in professional lockstep curricula, but the ethos of most programs is to keep with the herd and do what is expected. Professional students who request a semester or a year overseas are likely to be placed in the screwball box, or at a minimum be labeled eccentric.

Most of the structured opportunities for study abroad we encountered for students of business administration are either for one year exchange programs in Western Europe or for brief (and seemingly superficial) summer excursions to explore foreign commerce and industry. Neither was much favored by the faculty with whom we spoke; nor were they well constructed, it seemed to us, to prepare young managers in any depth for the challenges that lay ahead. A conspicuous exception is this joint-degree curriculum for students aiming for careers in business management at the University of Chicago Graduate School of Business.

The University of Chicago has exceptionally strong programs in international studies and a world-renowned business school. Flexibility and goodwill in both parts have led to the possibility of obtaining two Masters degrees – one in area studies or international relations and one in business administration – with very little extra cost and time. The M.B.A. curriculum at Chicago permits a student to complete the core business portion of the joint program with only fourteen quarter courses (three consecutive quarters) and a corresponding reduction in tuition from the nominal twenty-course equivalent. An additional nine courses satisfy requirements for the M.A., only three courses in total more than one M.B.A. alone. An "integrative research paper" demonstrating general competence in business and the chosen field of international studies is a final requirement of the joint program. Although study abroad is not spelled out as a requirement in the joint program, some form of foreign experience such as an extended internship is expected. Students have found these easy to arrange with foreign corporations.

This joint program was announced quietly only in 1985, but by the summer of 1986 fifteen students had enrolled. Applicants come from presently enrolled students in business and international studies and from outside the University. The goal is to equip a student aiming for a career in international business with the kind of integrated background for understanding the world from a professional perspective that is still rare in this country. In this case the joint initiative of the arts and sciences faculty and the business school are the key. The strong student response demonstrates the latent demand that almost certainly exists at other institutions as well.

7. Follow the markets overseas: the Lemberg Program in International Economics and Finance at Brandeis University

"Departmental" study abroad programs that incorporate overseas experience explicitly in a curriculum for a degree are relatively common in several areas of the humanities, such as the modern languages and history. In other areas, however, they are less familiar, and it may be useful to report on one innovative example here.

The Graduate School of Brandeis University recognizes the world economy as filled with important analytical and practical issues.

> With the expansion of international trade and the integration of world capital markets the field of international finance has become central to business decisions as well as public economic policy. Capital flows have grown phenomenally: the value of foreign exchange traded in New York in one week often equals the annual product of the American economy. Global markets, sources of supply, and options for borrowing

and investment are major sources of risk and opportunity to companies of all sizes. Public policy must also address the reality of interdependent markets. Beyond actions that directly affect foreign exchanges, a wide range of domestic industrial, technological, fiscal, and monetary policies are now recognized to have international repercussions and require consultation and coordination.

In addition the world economy has generated numerous employment opportunities for those with the right training.

Exciting careers are emerging in many branches of international business and policy. Lemberg graduates will be prepared for challenging positions in corporations with significant international interests, in securities trading and portfolio management, in investment houses, merchant banks, and other financial institutions, and in a variety of national and international governmental agencies. These jobs are very competitive and require talent, imagination, and drive. They also demand sophisticated training.

Brandeis has established a two-year Master's degree, in memory of a benefactor, designed to offer this training. Each class of about twenty-five students will take a selection of traditional courses in economics and management at Brandeis; but one semester of their four (usually the spring of the first year) will be spent in one of the leading universities in Denmark, England, France, Hong Kong, Israel, Italy, Japan, Mexico, Spain, or West Germany – studying the issues confronting a foreign economy and learning to view questions in business and policy from a non-American perspective. At the same time, the program at Brandeis hosts a number of students from abroad. The resulting mix of cultural and educational backgrounds helps to make the academic atmosphere at home lively, diverse, and truly international. This study abroad will be followed sometimes by an internship with a foreign firm or government agency. Material gathered during this internship may be the basis for the Master's project, presented during the spring of the second year. Proficiency in a modern foreign language is required. With the element of reciprocity so prominent, Brandeis can expect that the relationships with universities overseas may blossom under this program. Thus, even in as seemingly technical and focused a program as a Masters in International Economics and Finance, there is ample room for study abroad to make a major impact.

8. Take the world as your beat: programs in International Journalism at Baylor University and the University of Southern California

The media have been much criticized worldwide in recent years for failing to keep up in the quality of their news coverage with the range and complexity of international affairs. On issues of national security, social development, human rights, or economic relations they are likely as not to miss the real point. We encountered two Master's degree programs constructed to do something about this condition and which, although largely unknown to each other, are remarkably similar in purpose and structure. In both programs study abroad has a central role.

The founders and directors of these programs are both former foreign correspondents who had become deeply concerned about the state of foreign reporting and the paucity of knowledge of foreign correspondents. After having complained about it for some years, they felt compelled to do something about it themselves. Professor Loyal Gould at Baylor University directs a program for the degree of Master of International Journalism. He was a student visitor at the University of Heidelberg sometime after World War II, and left a career as an AP and NBC foreign correspondent because of his increasing sense that "experience as a police reporter seems today to be viewed by management of the media as the best training for reporting foreign news." He was influenced by Walter Lippmann's dictum that the best way to drive out incompetence is with competence; and to do so is now his goal.

The Baylor program is a professional journalism degree aimed at those who pursue careers in foreign correspondence or international news analysis. Gould believes that good journalism is simply applied research in the social sciences and humanities, and so he requires courses in these areas with only one integrative "international journalism seminar." Before graduation students must demonstrate "reading and spoken mastery of at least two languages (including English)" and pass an oral examination.

A critical part of the Baylor program is a "foreign journalism internship . . . six months spent within the student's foreign area of specialization and devoted to university work at a non-American institution, to employment with a U.S. or non-U.S. news organization, to independent study, or to a combination of all three: to an association with Southern Baptist mission posts, with public relations and advertising agencies, or with a wide range of foreign-based American firms."

Gould sees the internship as the high point of his program. He tries hard to obtain a balance of foreign and American students; and the latter go abroad for their internships, while the former either go abroad to a country other than their own or stay in the United States. Gould admits that finding just the right kind of foreign experience for each student is not easy, but he reports many successes. He gives as examples a French Canadian who spent time in South Africa; American students attached to the Asahi Shimbun in Tokyo, to a Nigerian news organization, and to the public relations division of a French firm; and Hong Kong and Japanese students working with Texas newspapers. He has even placed students at the Universities of Leningrad and Zagreb. One of his early graduates has won a Pulitzer Prize.

During our visit there were four foreigners and five Americans enrolled for the MIJ degree. A majority of the students have some journalistic experience already and, because of their varied backgrounds, they learn much from each other.

The University of Southern California program is directed by Murray Fromson, former foreign correspondent for the Associated Press and CBS News. Like Gould he brings to his task a missionary sense of the need for improvement in international journalism and ideas about how it can be done. The Center for International Journalism at USC was established in 1985 and the first students arrived in 1986. "The one year Master's program will emphasize the importance of language and area studies with an emphasis on the Third World." Generous support has been provided for the early years from external private sources. The Master's degree will be more highly structured than that at Baylor, with two semesters of "issue-oriented seminars and graduate level courses in international relations, history, political science and economics." Each year one or more regional foci will be announced, the first being Latin America. Between five and ten students are sought for each regional program. The third semester in the first program will be held at El Colegio de Mexico in Mexico City to "afford candidates an opportunity for some hands on experience: talks with government leaders, academicians, private citizens, representatives of public and lay opinion." Fluency in Spanish is required. Whereas the Baylor students are dispersed among regions and locations, for their period abroad the USC students will be kept together. At the conclusion of the first five years the USC Center hopes to have simultaneous programs operating for Latin America, the Pacific Rim, and the Middle East or Africa.

These two programs, both initiated by persons outside of traditional academe, represent unusually imaginative efforts to meet a well-accepted social need with graduate degree programs that incorporate study abroad as an essential component. It is not difficult to visualize how widely these experiments could be replicated in other fields. It is to be hoped that the well-known academic immune system does not react with sufficient vigor to expel these foreign bodies before they have had a chance to demonstrate their value conclusively.

9. Discovering the Northern Pacific: the North Pacific Program at the Fletcher School of Law and Diplomacy of Tufts University

It is commonplace to acknowledge the growing importance of the East Asian region in American life. For several years now the United States volume of trade with Asian states has exceeded its trade with Europe. Japan, South Korea, Singapore, Taiwan, and Hong Kong are not only some of our major trading partners but are among our fiercest competitors for world markets. Since World War II American combat forces, while perhaps best prepared to fight in Central Europe, have in fact fought in Korea and Vietnam. And, within the past decade, the prominence and energy of Asian Americans, from accomplished scientists to entrepreneurial food merchants, have become noted characteristics of our society. However, the study abroad programs in East Asia for American students remain spotty and, for the most part, are geared to the specialist – they are selective and a privilege rather than an entitlement. A notable exception to this trend is the North Pacific Program at The Fletcher School of Law and Diplomacy of Tufts University.

The Fletcher School, America's oldest graduate school of international affairs, has long trained generalists at the masters level (and relatively small numbers of specialists at the doctoral level) for careers in government service, international banking, and multinational corporations. Relatively few Fletcher graduates choose academic career paths. In 1983 Professor John Curtis Perry, a specialist in American–East Asian relations, established a program intended to interest students in the North Pacific region and its rimlands. Professor Perry has defined this region as the seven nations of Japan, China, the two Koreas, the Soviet Union, Canada, and the United States, "forming a great northern crescent that stretches from San Diego to Shanghai." The purpose of the program is "the study of the political, economic, and cultural currents of this region within both historical and current contexts."

As would be expected, the Fletcher School offers graduate seminars on Japanese, Korean, Chinese, and Russian civilization and foreign affairs. Starting in 1985 the North Pacific Program supplemented these substantial course offerings with an intensive two-week field seminar in Hokkaido, Japan. The seminar brought together ten Fletcher students and five faculty (about 20 percent of the Fletcher faculty) with counterparts from Japan, Canada, South Korea, and the People's Republic of China. The language of the seminar was English. Topics addressed by senior faculty included "The Sunbelt, the North Pacific, and the Reorientation of American Foreign Policy from East to West"; "The Pacific Shift in World Business How Far? How Fast? How North?"; and "Soviet Policy

Toward Japan." There were a wide variety of student presentations, student–faculty workshops, cultural activities, and keynote addresses by Dr. Zbigniew Brzezinski and former Canadian Prime Minister Pierre Trudeau. Funds for the program were provided by Japanese corporations, the Prefectural Government of Hokkaido, and the city of Sapporo, among others.

There are two especially interesting features of this program. First, there is a deliberate effort to develop a regional or multilateral (rather than bilateral) perspective. The collectivity of North Pacific nations is addressed rather than U.S.–Japan or Sino–American relations, as is often the case. Second, the program is aimed at the nonspecialist. It emphasizes study rather than research and is intended "to enrich the Fletcher experience for all those with an interest in that [North Pacific] part of the world."

A second seminar, with an expanded range of participants, including Soviets, was held in the summer of 1986 and a third in the summer of 1987. This third seminar had as its theme negotiating behavior in the region, and North Korean participants joined those from the other six nations that have been participating.

Fletcher also sends students for summer internships in Japan and Korea. Currently this involves five students who hold two-month summer positions in banks, universities, and government research institutes in Tokyo and Seoul. The students are paid a stipend by their sponsoring organization and their transpacific travel is covered by Fletcher. Eventually it is hoped that these experiences will be extended to a full year. The on-site learning by Fletcher students of Japanese corporate practices is a principal aim of this third phase of the program. In this Fletcher program study abroad involves graduate students with a professional orientation spending relatively short periods of time overseas. They are seeking to become educated about a set of cultures and a region of the world that will be central to their future careers without either conducting basic research or, for most of them, becoming linguistically proficient.

7

Where to go for help

It is all well and good to consider the objectives, the educational philosophies, the problems, and the alternative models that should be of central concern to any thoughtful planning of a study abroad program. It is quite another matter to collect the precise information and enlist the practical support of well-informed individuals who can assist senior administrators of an institution to get a study abroad program off the ground. This brief chapter is intended as a guide to the initiation of this daunting undertaking for those with a limited acquaintance with the major institutions and publications in the field.

Just as the previous chapters have demonstrated that there is no one objective of study abroad and no single "right" way to approach it, there is alas no unique repository of knowledge and advice on the subject that can provide all the answers to the sensible questions one can pose. Rather, for those interested in the initiation (or resuscitation) of a study abroad program it is wise to become acquainted with a variety of organizations and publications. Only by sampling from this professional smorgasbord can one determine the most appropriate mix of study abroad characteristics for a given institution.

To begin, a most useful reference for study abroad and other related organizations is *Global Guide to International Education*, edited by David Hoopes (New York: Facts on File Publications, 1984). This seven-hundred-page volume contains valuable capsule summaries of a multitude of U.S.- and foreign-based organizations and publications relevant to all aspects of international education, from the purposes of the American Hellenic Institute to the opportunities available for instruction in Yoruba. Even a cursory examination of its forty-page index of organizations, publications, and topics provides a useful overview of the range of activities in this field.

Using this volume as a general reference, it is possible to divide the relevant organizations and their publications into several types: national, regional, and independent.

National organizations

An obvious starting place to go for help about study abroad is the National Association for Foreign Student Affairs (NAFSA) at 1860 19th Street, N.W. in Washington, D.C. NAFSA is an extremely active and effective professional association for persons involved in all aspects of international educational exchange. Its members include administrators of study abroad programs, admissions officers, foreign student advisors, teachers of English as a second language, and others. NAFSA performs numerous functions: the provision of information and advice on various phases of international student affairs, in-service consultation and training programs for member institutions, the sponsoring of national and regional conferences, the publication of a variety of books, pamphlets, and bibliographies, and the maintenance of a large audiovisual library whose materials are available on loan. Among NAFSA's many publications, a useful guide is *Study Abroad: Handbook for Advisers and Administrators,* which delineates elements of the advisory process, the administration of the advisory office, and the operation of study abroad programs. The unit within NAFSA that is directly concerned with study abroad issues is the Section on U.S. Students Abroad (SECUSSA). Among its useful products, SECUSSA has published a *Bibliography on Study, Work, and Travel Abroad*, which offers a list of basic reference materials for guidance on study abroad.

One of the most useful aspects of NAFSA is the opportunity it provides for just plain networking, both nationally and within one of the twelve geographic "regions" that constitute the NAFSA regional membership structure. Unlike some automotive associations that will provide road maps to members only, advice about the fastest and safest route to success in study abroad administration is available from NAFSA without first paying a membership fee.

By plugging into the NAFSA network, it is possible to become informed in a relatively short time about everything from the basic mechanics of setting up an office to the overall philosophies about the role of study abroad that prevail at different types of institutions around the country. The first letter of inquiry or telephone call should be to the NAFSA central office, in Washington, D.C. The first question to ask is the name, address, and telephone number of the current chairperson of SECUSSA. Also handy to have is the name of the SECUSSA chairperson for the region where the institution in question is located: It could turn out to be a relatively short trip to his/her own campus, where a more thorough briefing can take place. These chairpersons will have lengthy experience in the field of study abroad and should be a gold mine of useful information. Of particular interest will be the opportunities NAFSA provides through regional seminars and workshops to newcomers; there is at least one such seminar somewhere in the country each year. In-service training and consultation programs provide "outreach" services to campuses just getting started in study abroad or seeking to revitalize this aspect of their academic offerings. Finally, the annual NAFSA regional and national conferences generally have many sessions devoted to the study abroad field and can be a worthwhile investment in time and money.

Among NAFSA's many useful publications in the study abroad field must be included the recently updated *Bibliography on Study Work and Travel Abroad*, *Study Abroad: A Handbook for Advisors and Administrators*, as well as a video on *Setting up the Study Abroad Office*.

A second major national organization is the Institute of International Education (IIE) at 809 United Nations Plaza in New York City, the largest non-profit service organization for postsecondary educational exchange. It administers U.S. government-sponsored graduate student grants (Fulbrights) as well as other U.S., foreign-government, and privately funded programs for overseas study. It serves as an informational clearinghouse on international exchange in postsecondary education and responds to phone and written inquiries from students, faculty, and staff of accredited educational institutions. IIE also maintains an International Education Information Center in its New York headquarters, where visitors can stop in and browse through a vast quantity of study and scholarship materials. It has a network of overseas offices that enhance its utility both for foreign students coming to study in the United States and for Americans studying abroad. Among its publications, IIE produces handbooks that are invaluable to study abroad advisors, principally *Academic Year Abroad*, *Vacation Study Abroad*, and *U.S. College-Sponsored Programs: Academic Year*. These are a compilation of study abroad programs sponsored by U.S. colleges and universities by continent, country, and city overseas. The volumes provide just enough information on each program listed to enable students and their advisors to get a feel for whether it's worth requesting further information and application forms. Descriptions include information on program length and dates, fields of study, language of instruction, housing options, eligibility requirements for admission, and costs.

In response to the demand for more information on opportunities in Great Britain, the IIE now publishes a volume entitled *Study in the United Kingdom and Ireland* with listings of British and Irish university programs to which students can apply, whether directly or through U.S. university study abroad program sponsors.

NAFSA and IIE have a multitude of services to foreign students in the United States, and they devote only a modest proportion of their effort to study abroad. The Council on International Educational Exchange (CIEE) at 205 East 42nd Street in New York City, on the other hand, is mainly occupied with travel and curriculum issues in study abroad. The CIEE has a membership of approximately 160 colleges, universities, and academic consortia and provides consultation and advisory services on educational exchange. The CIEE maintains overseas programs and study centers for U.S. academic consortia, which include the Cooperative Russian Language Program in Leningrad, the Inter-University Center for Films and Critical Studies in Paris, the China Cooperative Language and Studies Program, and many others. The purpose of these cooperative programs is to establish collective and collaborative efforts among a number of colleges and universities aimed at accomplishing together what a single institution would have difficulty achieving on its own. In 1986 the cooperative programs were united under the name Cooperative Centers for Study Abroad. At this writing there are twelve centers in six countries, jointly sponsored by five consortia of North American colleges and universities, and administered by the CIEE. Although each cooperative center is distinct, there are certain common characteristics: Sponsoring colleges and universities have full responsibilities for academic policy and curriculum development; programs and courses, once established, become part of the offerings of the home institutions; consortium member institutions provide academic credits and financial aid to participating students as though the students were in residence on the home campus; all centers have resident academic directors who provide day-to-day supervision; and consortium members are involved in an ongoing evaluation process through faculty and student assessments and program reviews. The CIEE is also especially active in arranging student travel services through the New York Student Center and Council Travel Services, Inc. These include general information, issuance of the International Student Identity Card, and low-cost overseas air, land, and group travel. CIEE publications of particular interest include *Work, Study and Travel Abroad: The Whole World Handbook* and *Wanted Abroad*, which is a free guide to work opportunities in five European countries. On balance, the CIEE is perhaps the most deeply committed and academically prestigious national organization concerned primarily with study abroad.

Some models for a modest beginning

For an institution wishing to make a modest start at little or no administrative cost one relatively safe approach is to "piggyback" students onto programs run by other U.S. universities and colleges. The IIE publications are the basic source of information about which programs will take students other than their own. Another shortcut is to send students through some of the organizations or associations that will place the students at universities around the world. For Great Britain, for example, the College Center for Education Abroad (CCEA), coordinated from Beaver College in Glenside, Pennsylvania, places qualified students from "feeder" schools around the country into British universities. Additional support services are provided by the CCEA before, during, and after the sojourn abroad, easing the burden for all concerned. For an American undergraduate to be successfully "mainstreamed" into any British university a good understanding of the differences between our two educational systems in general, and the variations between individual British universities in particular, is extremely important. Obtaining course descriptions to which academic advisors can relate can be an overwhelming problem for the inexperienced: Registrars tear their hair over the unfamiliar forms of documentation that arrive after the study abroad experience upon which an entire year's worth of credit is to be based. Dealing through programs such as the one run by Beaver College might well be worthwile, if only because they provide a voice at the end of the telephone for parents to yell at or complain to at various points.

A similar type of organization is the Institute of European Studies (IES) at 700 North Rush Street in Chicago. This organization places students into universities in France, West Germany, Italy, Austria, Spain, Mexico, Singapore, and Japan. At the same time, however, it maintains academic centers of its own at these sites where additional instruction is provided with an academic structure and pace that is familiar to the American student. In some of these centers (Vienna, Austria; Freiburg, West Germany; Nagoya, Japan) the instruction is in English, enabling students to experience the foreign language setting without this being an obstacle to higher-level course content.

Reciprocal exchange programs have many advantages but are highly labor-intensive to administer. For small institutions that wish to begin with an exchange or two with universities overseas, there is an organization called the International Student Exchange Program (ISEP) based at Georgetown University in Washington,

D.C. ISEP is a university exchange program open to students from member institutions. The central function of ISEP is to arrange reciprocal exchanges among more than 120 institutions in twenty countries in which participating students pay all expenses at their home institution and attend a host institution with no additional charge. Only full-time students or recent graduates of ISEP member institutions are eligible. Such exchanges normally last for a full academic year. Students are nominated by their home institutions to ISEP.

The scene overall

Beyond formal organizations such as these, there are a large number of informal networks among study abroad coordinators. A group from northeastern colleges and universities, for example, meets regularly twice a year to exchange views on such topics as the impact of study abroad programs on admissions in their respective institutions, the methodologies for granting credit for study abroad, and trends in policies that permit students to take their scholarship aid with them when they study abroad.

It should be evident that there is a wide variety of institutions and individuals in the study abroad community who are available to assist institutions that wish to establish study abroad programs of their own or link up with others. There is a burgeoning literature on the subject and a great deal of enthusiasm and expertise available at the local, regional, and national levels.

This review has meant to be suggestive rather than definitive, and is intentionally more descriptive than evaluative. None of the organizations cited above were themselves subject to evaluation in this study; rather the purpose in offering this information is to reflect the rich diversity of services, programs, and literature available to those who seek to become better acquainted with study abroad.

It is best not to go it alone

Certain features of the world of study abroad impressed us in particular: It is extremely complex; it is fast moving; and the risks encountered are very great. For these reasons alone we strongly urge participation in cooperative activities of all kinds. There is simply too much for any persons working alone to master, and the dangers of spending time reinventing wheels are very great. The loner in the world of study abroad is likely not only to miss opportunities that appear suddenly on the national scene but also to remain unattuned to dangerous currents in individual countries and on the larger world stage. Those responsible for study abroad on any campus should themselves travel. They should gain first-hand exposure to the national organizations that can serve them – ideally by personal visits but at a minimum by telephone – and should visit some of the programs to which they send students overseas (just as one should test the guest-room bed by sleeping in it oneself). National and regional meetings should also be attended, especially those of NAFSA and SECUSSA.

Finally, because study abroad is still such a vibrant young field in America, much can be gained from informal local interactions – rather like pioneers on the frontier working together to put up a barn. We were impressed by the number of examples of cooperative endeavors we saw on our travels, such as groups of advisors or admissions officers who meet across a state or region to compare notes, plot collaborative projects, and just give each other a sense of mutual support, like new homesteaders out there on the prairies.

As it turns out there are lots of places to go for help. Anyone who does not seek it is simply ill-advised.

8

Conclusion and recommendations

Ever since the end of World War II the leaders of American higher education have been proposing to "internationalize" their institutions. The means they have employed, in successive waves, have been as follows:

1. beginning in the 1950s, service to the nation (via the Federal Government and private foundations) through the administration of technical assistance contracts overseas;
2. from the 1960s onward the development of strong area studies programs;
3. especially from the 1970s, the offer of a warm welcome to large numbers of foreign students on their campuses; and finally
4. an explosion of study abroad especially in the 1980s.

There are tides in the affairs of American colleges and universities (to extend a metaphor used extensively in the discussions above), and there is little doubt that institutions must catch them and ride the waves, lest they be washed under and ultimately rest becalmed. But "surf's up," so best be moving. This book is designed to assist leaders of colleges and universities to know the waves, polish their surfboards, and rejoice in the sport.

The object lessons at hand

What are some of the precise lessons to be drawn from this report on study abroad in American higher education during the 1980s? Certain conclusions may be reached for colleges and universities as a whole. Others will apply only to specific institutions and must be inferred by persons who know these institutions well.

Above all, leaders of American academe should recognize that this is a fast-moving field that they ignore at their peril. If they do not act to their own advantage in a timely fashion, not only will they miss opportunities but their competitors will surpass them. The continued dynamism of the field is so great that a laggard institution cannot simply say, "Let's wait till the dust clears and then pick the best." The dust shows no sign of settling any time soon, and if an institution is not in there with the others who are stirring it up, it will have little opportunity to gain the understanding needed for sensible action later on.

Second, it must be grasped clearly that today study abroad is a dimension of higher education that should be taken into account across the full breadth of educational programs and institutions. The conception that study abroad is for rich young women in the humanities at private colleges who wish to spend time in Europe, or for promising young men selected for Rhodes or Marshall scholarships, has no validity today – if it ever had any even in the earlier days. An educational experience overseas may be the best way to develop the culturally sensitive person at any level and anywhere. The full potential of this practice will be achieved only when study abroad can no longer even be conceived as a separate phenomenon, but is integrated fully within our conception of education. In Chapter 3 we discussed nineteen potential objectives for overseas study; undoubtedly there are more. But old myths and prejudices die slowly and educational leaders may have to lean hard on their colleagues to look fairly and squarely at all of the possible benefits and all of the options before them. Many of the most exciting opportunities for major contributions lie in the sciences, the professional schools, and graduate study generally. Yet, paradoxically, in most institutions these are the most conservative elements and the slowest to take such an unfamiliar opportunity as study abroad very seriously. We hope that perhaps the few examples we have provided of imaginative departures that have occurred in some places already may stimulate more creativity elsewhere.

What is truly unique about this fourth round in the internationalizing of higher education is that everyone can play. By and large only strong and complex universities could take part in technical assistance and develop strong area studies programs. The growth of foreign student populations depends substantially on the eccentric tastes of these students to go into this field rather than that one, or to live in one region rather than another. But all kinds of institutions can and do send their students overseas. We saw some of the most and least exciting applications in virtually every category of institution we visited. We saw imaginative and successful programs in some small liberal arts and community colleges as well as in some major research universities; but we also saw little at all in others. The constraints on actions of institutions in this area arise from the limitations of their own will and vision rather than from resources alone or from the structural category in which they find themselves.

The third lesson is that any institution must recognize that, in addition to a multitude of potential purposes that may be served by overseas study, today there is an abundance of ways to go about it. In Chapter 4 we have tried to suggest that the many different modes we uncovered need not be seen as stark alternatives from which one or two must be selected, but instead as a rich cafeteria or menu from which a full well-balanced meal of complementary dishes may be put together. Indeed we find it nicely symmetrical that the wide range of objectives spelled out in Chapter 3 can in fact be matched by the full array of instruments discussed in Chapter 4.

The fourth lesson to be learned is that study abroad, when done well, is not easy. There are many tasks that require careful attention if the full benefits of the programs are to be obtained, and in the worst case for disaster to be avoided. Just as the list of goals and structural modes we provided are not necessarily complete, the specific tasks we have outlined in Chapter 5 are not intended to be exhaustive; but they should give a sense of the range and complexity of the work to be done. From even a quick perusal of these tasks it must be evident that the effective operation of overseas study requires skill, effort, and commitment throughout the institution.

A fifth lesson is that perhaps the greatest hazard facing study abroad on any campus is that it will become merely another marginal appendage of the educational enterprise, consigned to a remote administrative home and a physical location far from the center of action. This condition cuts off the study abroad process from its lifeblood, to which it contributes as well as draws sustenance, and consigns it to near-certain oblivion sooner or later. In the event of one of the crises that regularly ensue, study abroad cannot survive as part of the marginalia. But even more important than this perilous condition that is created, marginal status prevents a campus from taking full advantage of the rich benefits that should accrue from the extended horizons provided by this new window on the world.

The integration of study abroad should occur along two dimensions: First, study abroad should be related closely to other international activities on campus, especially area studies, international affairs programs, technical assistance, and foreign students on campus. The opportunities for synergism are obvious and the costs of isolation are considerable. An effort to examine international education on campus in a comprehensive fashion should be a high priority.

Second, study abroad must be integrated fully into the educational process and not be treated as an unconnected diversion. Students who will study abroad should be encouraged to plan for it early. They should be counseled on language study and curriculum as soon as possible in their careers. There should be a predeparture orientation appropriate for the type of study contemplated. Following a student's return to campus the foreign experience should be used and thereby strengthened in every practicable way. A reentry seminar should be explored, but at a minimum returnees should be asked to build on the experience in classes, seminars, and theses. The costs of ignoring the effects of overseas study on a student are both loss of the positive results and a feeling of alienation from the home campus.

The sixth lesson is that there are cycles, trends, rhythms, and other dynamic features associated with study abroad that should not cause too much surprise or concern – just as there are with many aspects of higher education. Typically a program begins with a substantial level of enthusiasm on a campus where it has not thrived before. At the start the benefits often shine more brightly than the problems. Over time, however, the difficulties become ever more apparent, and skepticism grows – the "antibodies" gain strength. If the initial growth period is not used to integrate the program thoroughly and to provide solid community backing, the entire movement may "die aborning." This is by no means to suggest that long-run success is exceptional. We encountered numerous cases where, despite vicissitudes, viability has never been in doubt and permanence seemed ensured from the beginning. In one unusual case an extended longitudinal research project that supplemented instruction, and for which successive generations of students gathered data, provided a cumulative sense of value and permanence to the entire enterprise.

Perhaps the final lesson to be gained from this report is that study abroad is today truly a new frontier of higher education. This places a high premium on the frontier spirit, on the contributions of the explorer-entrepreneur, on Daniel Boone as well as on Columbus and Lewis and Clark. Educational leaders, like Queen Isabella and the thirteen colonies, need to be ready to take advantage of opportunities when they arise and to be prepared for some failures along the way. It will all be worthwhile in the end.

Specific advice to campus CEOs

It may be helpful for us to spell out in this final section a list of the actions that we believe should be taken at a minimum by campus authorities so as to take full advantage of the opportunities presented by overseas study. These suggestions have all been discussed in detail in the body of the report. They are simply drawn together here as a convenient checklist.

1. Provide unambiguous leadership

For many campuses serious overseas study would be a major innovation and departure. Such a change of direction does not happen anywhere without clear demonstration of interest and commitment at the top. The first step to be taken is a strong policy statement in an important public address or campus report. This must be followed up with action and allocation of resources. If appropriate the governing board should endorse the institutional commitment as well. Talk is cheap, and president-watchers look closely to distinguish public relations statements from serious operationally specific calls to action. Committed leadership from the campus CEO will almost certainly be required to effect and sustain the integration of study abroad into the overall international thrust of the institution. Up until now one of the main sources of weakness in study abroad programs on many campuses has been the attitude of faculty who view education anywhere off campus, and especially overseas, with suspicion or hostility. Study abroad can never truly prosper or fulfil its great promise without a change in this attitude. Only the faculty can plan effectively facilities and implement successful study abroad; but such a change in attitude can be accomplished only by the campus leaders.

2. Conduct campuswide inquiry to establish goals and preferred modes

Study abroad deserves close scrutiny on any campus from the most thoughtful and imaginative members of the community. Moreover, it is a subject full of interesting questions and puzzles that hold the attention of competent people. After announcing a meaningful commitment to study abroad a campus leader should invite a "blue-ribbon" committee of respected campus citizens to address a range of questions of the kind raised especially throughout Chapters 3–6. Their report should be widely circulated and discussed. The committee should, above all, contain not just friends and advocates of study abroad: For any activity involved as centrally as this in the academic programs to prosper it must gain the respect or at least the acquiescence of the unconverted. Let them be represented fully in the inquiry.

3. Sustain high-level interest

Following the campuswide inquiry a continuing committee of oversight of study abroad programs should be named. This may include some members of the blue-ribbon committee of inquiry, but in the same way it should not represent principally the special interests associated with study abroad. The oversight committee is to perform several critical functions: It passes judgment on program development at the highest level. It helps administrators to remember what is truly important, and thereby retains the confidence of the faculty in what is happening. (In this respect it performs the function of a faculty council for a college or school.) In addition the oversight committee, representing the entire academic community, may serve as a crucial defender of study abroad in the event of the crises, financial and substantive, that are bound to occur. Without this group of sympathetic and informed, yet also detached, campus citizens, study abroad stands politically naked and nearly defenseless before its skeptics.

This committee should have the charge, and the clout, to make all relevant parts of the institution face up to issues of study abroad, to consider the advantages as well as the costs, and to explore the examples set by others. The committee cannot, of course, impose its will on any unwilling educational units, but it should be able to make them sit up and think and defend their positions.

4. Maintain detailed supervision

In addition to maintenance of high-level oversight, it is necessary to watch carefully and rule upon many of the details of study abroad, both for programs operated by the home campus and for external programs patronized by home campus students. Someone must discern what is the true content of these programs and make this information known. To what are they equivalent in campus programs? Should transfer credit be awarded? If so, in what form? Should warnings about quality be issued to certain programs, and if so which and what? Apart from the ethical questions involved, educational administrators should be especially alert to responsibilities under truth-in-advertising for all aspects of study abroad. Failure to do so may come back to haunt them and their governing boards for years to come. These are the kinds of questions and issues that require sustained attention from skilled and dedicated experts. A committee with a different membership from the oversight committee is required. Persons with the requisite competence and interest for this second committee are likely to be present or former directors of undergraduate instruction in departments, registrars, and assistant deans of professional schools.

5. Establish an effective administrative structure

There is no way to prescribe in general for the administrative requirements of institutions of many different sizes, shapes, financial circumstances, and purposes, but certain dos and don'ts may be suggested. The director of study abroad should be a person of breadth, sympathy, intelligence, experience, and stature on campus. This is not an appropriate burying ground for an unsuccessful tenure candidate, an obsolete faculty member, or an incompetent functionary from somewhere else in the institution. This position should be thought of as an appealing stepping stone for higher administrative office and should attract the talent commensurate with this destiny.

The administration of study abroad should, in most cases at least, be lodged within the academic administration reporting directly to the academic vice-president or provost to symbolize its institutionwide responsibilities. Close links must be sustained with the undergraduate college, perhaps through some dual title and reporting responsibilities. In addition contact must be formed and nurtured with student affairs, the other schools in the institution, the registrar, student aid, and the business office. Moreover, close coordination between study abroad offices and foreign student advisory activities tends to strengthen both functions.

6. Face the resource issue squarely

No distinguished study abroad program will be costless; but it should not be extremely expensive over the long haul. One of the critical financial problems faced by overseas programs is short-term variability in costs and revenues. It should not be beyond the capabilities of an imaginative administrator to deal with this condition. One approach may be to decide how much net subsidy will be allocated to study abroad over an extended time period – say, $200,000 per year over five years – and then provide the director and oversight committee with this amount of resources at the start on the understanding that there is no more where that came from over the full period. This working capital fund will guarantee survival over lean years and will permit sensible financial behavior overall. The opportunities for external assistance to study abroad from foundations, corporations, and individuals should be fully explored.

7. Arrange for periodic external evaluation

Most campuses have a regular procedure for review of academic units. Implementation of such a procedure is especially important for study abroad. In such a fast-moving field as this, either an ad hoc committee of assessment or a permanent visiting committee with rotating membership, meeting at specified intervals, can serve two critical functions. If the members are carefully chosen, it can keep the local study abroad community in touch with national developments, and it can advise the senior administration about what is working and what is not, and why. External evaluation of this kind enables an institution to learn from and share with others and it establishes reasonable standards by which programs may be judged.

We confidently expect that a decade hence there will be no need for a book of this kind. By that time the place of study abroad on the American campus will be as well understood as that of the graduate school, library, or football team. In the meantime we trust that we have helped to open the subject to those who have not had occasion to think hard about it. We hope that the long-run effect will be that more students will be able to benefit from this vital new dimension of their higher education. In sum, we have not sought here to provide the answers. We have, however, endeavored to raise the big questions, summarize how some institutions have answered them, and suggest approaches for constructive responses to this increasingly significant endeavor.

Appendix: institutions visited

I. California

1. California State University, Long Beach
2. Claremont Graduate School, Claremont
3. Los Angeles Community College, Los Angeles
4. Pomona College, Claremont
5. Stanford University, Palo Alto
6. University of California, Berkeley
7. University of California, Los Angeles
8. University of California, Santa Barbara
9. University of California, Santa Cruz
10. University of Southern California, Los Angeles

II. Illinois

1. Chicago Loop College, Chicago
2. Knox College, Galesburg
3. Lake Forest College, Lake Forest
4. Northwestern University, Evanston
5. Rockford College, Rockford
6. University of Chicago, Chicago
7. University of Illinois, Champaign/Urbana
8. University of Northern Illinois, DeKalb

III. Massachusetts

1. Boston College, Chestnut Hill
2. Boston University, Boston
3. Brandeis University, Waltham
4. Harvard University, Cambridge
5. Massachusetts Institute of Technology, Cambridge
6. Mount Holyoke College, South Hadley

7. Smith College, Northampton
8. Tufts University, Medford
9. University of Massachusetts, Amherst

IV. New York

1. College Consortium on International Studies, New York
2. Institute of International Education, New York

V. Texas

1. Austin Community College, Austin
2. Baylor University, Waco
3. Rice University, Houston
4. Southern Methodist University, Dallas
5. Texas A&M, College Station
6. Texas Southern University, Houston
7. Trinity University, San Antonio
8. University of Dallas, Dallas
9. University of Texas, Austin

VI. Washington, D.C.

1. Council for International Exchange of Scholars

Index